Michael Waeber / Hans Steinbichler

Valais East

48 selected day walks
round Zermatt, Saas, Fiesch,
Brig and Simplon
as well as a 6-day round walk through the Matter valley
and a 3-day walk from the Rhône valley
over the Simplon pass to Gondo

With 57 colour photos, 49 1:50.000 walking maps,
one 1:100.000 walking map
as well as a 1:800.000 contextualising map

Translated by Gill Round

ROTHER • MUNICH

Frontispiece:
The Weißhorn from Tufteren ridge path.
Photo: Michael Waeber

Picture opposite title page (Page 2):
Late autumn in the Valais.
Photo: Hans Steinbichler

Acknowledgment of photos (page numbers):
Herbert Kunstmann (93).
All other pictures by the authors.

Cartography:
© Bergverlag Rother, Munich
1 : 800.000 overview map © Freytag & Berndt, Vienna

Translation: Gill Round

1st edition 2001
© Bergverlag Rother GmbH, München

ISBN 3-7633-4806-9

Distributed in Great Britain by Cordee, 3a De Montfort Street, Leicester
Great Britain LE1 7HD, www.cordee.co.uk
in USA by AlpenBooks, 3616 South Road, C-1, Mukilteo,
WA 98275 USA, www.alpenbooks.com

ROTHER WALKING GUIDES

Creta West · Iceland · La Palma · Mallorca · Mont Blanc · Norway South · Provence · Sardinia ·
Valais East · Around the Zugspitze

**Dear mountain lovers! We would be happy to hear your opinion and
suggestions for amendment to this Rother Walking guide.**

BERGVERLAG ROTHER · Munich
D-85521 Ottobrunn · Haidgraben 3 · Tel. 0049/89/608669-0 · Fax -69
Internet http://www.rother.de · E-mail bergverlag@rother.de

Preface

The Valais, land of the highest peaks, long glaciers, steep slopes and gorge-like valleys, is a real walkers' paradise. Many of the narrow and steep-sided valleys open out higher up and the slopes are covered with green meadows and forests. Alpine huts stand in fantastic locations with distant views, and barns and storehouses close by. The latter, on their six or nine stilts, are covered by large stone slabs, the so-called »Mäusesteine«, (mouse stones). Ancient, pleasantly located paths lead up from the valley bottom or from high-lying settlements – paths which were only constructed for walkers, with no thought to wheeled transport at the time of building. And every one of these alpine pastures has its neighbour, higher up, further below or on the same slope, separated by steep slopes and ravines. They not only make links with the valley below but connect with the high peaks on the other side of the valley along paths which are often marvellous viewing terraces. Like ridge paths, the enjoyment of walking along these terraces is the little variation in height. Other highlights are routes along old water channels, the Suonen, which used to bring water to the dry meadows and fields and some of them are still in use today. There is wonderful walking on paths in exquisite locations across steep hillsides beside babbling streams.

Many of the highest peaks in the Alps are to be found in the Valais. There are mountaineers here from all around the world walking from high-lying huts up to the big peaks. There are paths to all of these Swiss Alpine Club huts and they are renowned as ideal for hiking, with some justification.

This guide to the »Valais East« presents the reader with 50 suggestions for walks in the German speaking part of the mountain canton. A second volume, the »Valais West«, provides just as many in the French speaking part. The Raspille stream, which flows into the Rhône between Salgesch and Sierre from north, marks the language boundary. The walks go across the flanks of the Rhône valley or in its side valleys. No special equipment is necessary for these walks. Experience in walking along narrow and some-times also exposed sections is an advantage. Some of the walks are easy, being suitable for family outings and now and then mountain bikes can also be used. A lot of help was given to us in compiling the selection of walks and for this, thanks must go to: our walking companions who tolerated many »extra walks« for the purpose of taking photos, the men and women working in the tourist offices who helped us with information and their experience. Thanks also to the Swiss Post Office (PTT), the Swiss railways (SBB) as well as several local mountain railway companies. We wish the users of this guide many days in the Valais, full of sunshine and adventure.

Michael Waeber
Hans Steinbichler

Contents

Abbreviations:

BVZ	Zermatt Railway
BLS	Bern-Lötschberg-Simplon Railway
FO	Furka-Oberalp Railway
PTT	Swiss Post (post, telegraph, telephone)
SAC	Swiss Alpine Club
SBB	Swiss National Railway

Tourist tips

Use of the guide

The suggestions for walks are generally arranged from east to west, ie westwards from the Goms as far as the language boundary at the Raspille. Walks into the side valleys are listed under the name of the appropriate valley, the only exceptions being where some paths, adjacent to each other, need to be described in the same section for your convenience. Place names are usually according to the Swiss spelling. Tourist and cultural information about the locations is summarised in the following chapter. A collection of possible alternative activities for »rainy days and rest days' can be found in the »bad weather chapter«.

The most important information for each walk is presented in dossier-like form, together with the accessibility of the starting points by public transport (Switzerland serves as a model, in this respect). After a short characterisation of the walk there's the route description. A colour walking map provides you with a good overview and the colour photo too gives an impression of the region. In the index at the back you will find all the mountain ranges mentioned, the locations, starting points, bases and objectives for every stage. The walks can be easily located with the help of the contextualising map on page 35.

Grade

All the walks described in the guide are easy and can be undertaken with the relevant mountaineering equipment (sturdy shoes and appropriate clothing) often into late autumn. This does not mean that sure-footedness and a good head for heights are never required. In order to assess the demands more accurately the suggestions for walks are marked with different colours. They are as follows:

BLUE

The paths are good and marked throughout. They are sufficiently wide and only moderately steep, and relatively safe, even in poor weather. These walks can also be undertaken by children and older people without any great difficulty.

RED

These paths are sufficiently marked, but for the most part narrow and somewhat exposed in some places. Some short stretches of path may also be made safe with cables and should only be undertaken by sure-footed mountain walkers with the right equipment.

An arctic-like picture: Märjelen lake at the Aletsch glacier (Walk 11).

BLACK
These paths are also sufficiently marked, usually narrow and with some lengthy steep sections. In places they can be very exposed and you will need to use your hands sometimes. This means that these walks should only be attempted by totally sure-footed and fit hikers with alpine experience.

Dangers
Almost all the walks follow well marked paths. Reference is made in the text to places which are particularly exposed or demanding. Some routes go over the 3000m mark and you have to be prepared for snow, even in summer. In doubtful conditions it is best to make inquiries in the valley (eg. in the tourist and guide offices) or walk round the area first on lower paths.

Equipment

Most important piece are suitable shoes with sturdy soles – so-called trekking boots have proved to be successful. Long comfortable trousers, warm and protective clothing, hat and gloves for high altitude routes, in summer as well, (and even when it's hot in the valley in high summer). For autumn, when the days are getting shorter, it is recommended that you carry a head-torch. You should, of course, take sufficient to drink with you (not in environmentally unfriendly cans, but in your own water bottles) and also enough to eat.

Maps

Many of the walks can be undertaken by using the sections of map in this book. However it is recommended that you equip yourself with the excellent Swiss topographical maps (a map of the whole of Switzerland or special regional ones put together by the tourist associations). These elaborate works of art, with their clarity and detail, are the most useful for countless other projects. The prices are about 13 SFr for the normal maps, the individual maps with walking routes and concise path descriptions are priced according to size, from 10 to 25 SFr. They are available from book shops, kiosks, railway stations and tourist offices.

Walking times

There are basic problems about giving time details. In this guide you are given the average length of time normally expected for each walk without having done any great »training«, and not including rests and photo stops! The times are simply an aid to planning. If, in good conditions, you are out for longer, then presumably you are getting more out of these walks. Basically, your schedule should be determined by the weather, the times of buses and trains or the approaching nightfall and not by your enthusiasm for setting new walking records.

Stops and accommodation

In this section you will find the restaurants and huts along the routes which are open in summer. Overnight stops are mentioned where available. For safety reasons in early summer or autumn you should inquire about the facilities in the valley. The restaurants or kiosks at the mountain stations are usually open during hours of operation.

Aiding your ascent

Cable-cars, lifts and taxi busses have been integrated into the routes where appropriate. Some services only operate in summer (all train and bus routes are contained in the Valais timetable, available in tourist offices and at train and bus ticket offices). If these railways are closed in autumn the walks might be longer, but they are quieter too!

Getting there
Some of the most famous Swiss alpine passes emerge in the Valais. As a result this region can be reached by car or post bus from practically every direction – over the Grimsel and the Furka passes from central Switzerland, the Nufenen pass from the Tessin, the Simplon pass from the Lago-Maggiore region, the Great St. Bernard pass from the Aosta valley as well as the Col de Forclaz coming east from Chamonix. Those in a hurry can take the motorway from Lake Geneva up as far as Sierre. It is also useful, not only in winter, to be able to take the car on the train through the Lötschberg tunnel from the Bern region and beneath the furka pass from Realp/Andermatt.
The valley is, however, also very well connected to the international railway network. Consequently there are amongst others, through trains from Paris, Brussels, Milan and various German towns which make for an effortless and restfull journey. If you would really like to treat yourself, you can undertake a real holiday trip to the Valais with the Glacier Express from Chur or St. Moritz. The Lötschberg line, too, from the Thuner lake in the Bernese uplands is an experience in itself due to its amazing route! And, continuing by train or bus is just as easy once in the Valais since a frequent service connects not only the larger villages, but practically every valley as well.

Protection of nature and the environment.
We should stress at this point the need for care in protecting nature. This wonderful landscape, in parts still the same as it was thousands of years ago, but also shaped by many centuries of human use, is after all what the holiday maker is looking for and wants to find in the future. Especially on holiday one ought to be able to do without anything which results in pollution of the environment, excessive use of energy as well as the disruption of cultivation and inhabitants. Therefore, leave everywhere as you would wish to find it, by using the least amount of packaging (walkers should take back to the valley all litter and duly dispose of it there) and of course by limiting the production of »air litter« with sparing use of the car. Of all holiday activities« walking offers the most intensive contact with nature, but is ideal, even in the age of mass tourism, for showing people what is worth protecting in the most environmentally friendly way.
Unfortunately the degradation of the landscape which walkers find in all parts of the Alps have to be confronted in the Valais as well. In particular we should mention downhill skiing for which whole valley communities have been sacrificed for the cabling and excavation of vast areas. Villages and mountain

settlements, having evolved harmoniously, have been transformed into city-like hotel and apartment complexes. 20 storey high-rise buildings have also made their way onto the alpine meadows. But the worse thing is that there still seems to be no end to the development in sight. The running sore of ski lifts is eating its way further and further into the remotest valleys and if the landscape and the climate do not suit, bulldozers and snow blasters lend a helping hand and make everything possible. When there is snow on the ground the winter visitor experiences an apparently intact world, but then the wounds become obvious in summer. Of course, at present, the big money is still being spent in winter and for many places this is seemingly the only possible means of survival, but for how much longer can we afford this type of holiday with its exhaustive use of energy and the landscape?

Happily some of the problems created by earlier attitudes towards alpine holidays are no longer being ignored. People do not escape from the hostile environment of the city to then rediscover it in a holiday resort. Already some places have begun to correct former sins by making an enormous capital investment, eg. to rebuild roads and resting places. Perhaps the mountain walker can provide an example, less harmful to nature, to skiing tourism and encourage a middle way between the total impoverishment of valley communities which have been dependent on tourism and a »techno-world« à la Val d'Isère. Also the tourist business is complying with the principles of supply and demand. Downhill skiing is as popular as ever and correspondingly the supply is good! Those responsible for tourism must be aware of the fact that the demands of the winter sportsman on a region are difficult to reconcile with the wishes of other visitors throughout the year.

Every single person can remind their host of the demand for an unspoilt landscape – with conversations, expressing their own wishes in the tourist office and lively discussion of environmental problems. Perhaps then, even you will have made a contribution to the decision by the inhabitants in future projects, to place more importance again on nature (ultimately their own basis for life) and less on making a fast buck. The Binn valley is a happy example of this.

The Weißhorn from the Tufteren ridge path in autumn (Walk 32).

Locations

In practically every place in the Valais you have a large choice of accommodation of all categories, whether it be hotels, b&b or holiday flats, all too numerous to mention. Prices are comparable with those in other parts of the Alps. It is of course advisable to book early in high season as it is everywhere, however in early summer and autumn there are sufficient vacancies. Campsites and group accommodation are pointed out since they are not available everywhere. The listing of tourist facilities cannot, of course, lay claim to being complete, nor can all villages be named for reasons of space – individual tourist offices will gladly be able to give further information. The height locations given of smaller places relate to the central point (church, station), but with settlements which are spread out, particularly those on hillsides, the height of the area is given. The upper Rhône valley is called »Goms«.

Gletsch, 1757m
A settlement, only inhabited in summer, with views of the Rhône glacier tongue which, barely 100 years ago, still came close to the houses. Nature trail in the glacial retreat area. Grimsel pass turn off from the Furka pass road. Permanent exhibition in the Belvedère hotel, mostly literature about the Valais, glacial cave. The Furka rack-railway which shut down at the beginning of the 80s is being restored at great expense and is expected to be in service from Realp to Gletsch from 1999 onwards and the opening of the section Oberwald to Gletach has been planned for 2002.

Oberwald, 1368m – Unterwassern, 1377m
Station of the Furka-Oberalp railway, car transport to Realp through the Furka tunnel. Highest village in the Rhône valley, inhabited all year round, with numerous possibilities for walking, chair-lift to the Hungerberg, Interesting baroque church. Group accommodation, campsite. Tourist information, tel: 027/9733232.

Obergesteln, 1355m
Obergesteln is an exception to the wooden architectural style prevalent in the eastern Valais and has stone buildings typical of the southern Alps, built after a great fire completely destroyed it in the middle of the 19th century. Castle, painting in the cemetery chapel, crystal museum, group accommodation.

Ulrichen, 1346m
Pretty place in the Upper Goms at the start of the Nufenenstraße, the highest Swiss mountain pass road, with rows of beautiful old houses. Wooden

houses dominate here as almost everywhere in the Valais, larch wood becomes a typical blackish-brown colour over the course of the years. Worth noticing are the small cornfields on the sunny slopes of the region, a contrast to the scale of fields of modern agriculture. New Gothic church from 1895. Group accommodation, campsite.

Geschinen, 1351m – Münster, 1388m

A cluster of villages with well-preserved wooden houses and barns. Münster church from 1491 (the tower is supposed to date from the 12th century), the famous high altar inside, carved in 1509. A little above, on the Biel, St. Antonius chapel. Parish museum. Tennis, rafting on the Rotten (the name of the Rhône in Goms), fishing, group accommodation. Associated tourist offices of Upper Goms, 3985 Münster, tel: 027/9731745.

Reckingen, 1326m – Überrotte, 1317m

Reckingen is situated north of the Rotten, having the effect of being a unified village, but it also continues above the road with very beautiful houses of dark larch wood. Right by the station there is an old covered wooden bridge over the Rotten which connects Überrotte – situated at the confluence of the Binne with the Rotten. Baroque church, perhaps the most splendid construction of its type in the Valais, with beautiful organ dating from 1745/46. Heated outdoor pool, horse riding and minigolf. Campsites, group accommodation. Tourist information 3998 Reckingen, tel: 027/9741216.

Gluringen, 1322m

Small village, just a short way up from the main road, church dating from the 15th century, horse riding.

Ritzingen, 1318m – Biel, 1312m – Selkingen, 1318m

These 3 places (Biel diocese) on the valley road have evolved almost as one. Ritzingen spreads a little way up the sunny slope, the other 2 are a unified cluster of villages with beautiful houses. Pilgrimage chapel (1687) on the Ritzinger Feld. The Biel parish church was enlarged in 1654, gothic tabernacle. Markus chapel in Selkingen with altar from 1678. Group accommodation, camping on the other side of the Rotten.

Blitzingen, 1297m – Bodmen, 1257m

Blitzingen had to be completely rebuilt after the fire in 1932 when only the church survived. The valley road goes below the village. The new holiday chalet complex Chastebiel goes northwards up the slope above the village. Bodmen on the other side of the Rotten has been able to preserve its old style as a narrow collection of old houses. There's no space for cars and parking is at the bridge just before the village.

View from above Ferden into the Lötschen valley (Walk 47).

Niederwald, 1251m

This village is especially picturesque since the old houses are still in good condition.

Bellwald (Bodmen – Eggen – Ried), 1340 – 1700m

Holiday resort on the ridge between the Fiesch and Rhône valleys with magnificent views, beautiful village centre (Baroque church from 1610), many new buildings and opportunities for walking, eg the Gommer ridge path. Chairlift via Fleschen to Steibenkreuz under the Risihorn. Cable-car and connection by road from Fürgangen above Fiesch (FO stop). Tennis, mini-golf, group accommodation. Tourist information 3997 Bellwald, tel: 027/9711684.

Fiesch, 1251m – Fiesch valley, 1030 – 1180m

Situated at the confluence of the Fiesch and Rhône valleys. Since the start of this century, the economic centre point of the Goms with the building of the railway – the traffic had previously gone on the other side of the valley through Ernen. Beautiful old renovated houses have been maintained despite many new buildings. The St. Antonius chapel (1691), is in the hamlet of Wichel, in Wiler the Trinity chapel from 1703. Holiday centre: large sport centre (swimming pool, tennis, squash, minigolf, sports' halls), Eggishorn cable-car, walkers' paradise, hang-gliding and paragliding. Training centre for mountaineers. Group accommodation. Tourist information 3984 Fiesch, tel: 027/9711466.

Ernen, 1195m – Mühlebach, 1248m – Steinhaus, 1269m

Ernen is known, well beyond its borders, for its historical village which has not altered for over 100 years due to a strict ruling about new houses. In the church (beginning of the 16th century) there's an interesting collection of valuable art objects and the still exemplary organ dating from 1680. Ernen is regarded as a village of music, every year there are organ weeks and international chamber orchestral courses as well as many concerts. Steinhaus and Mühlebach are small settlements, still largely in their original state, the St. Josefs chapel from 1676 is on »Biel« hill, more or less a symbol of Mühlebach. The road from Ernen-Mühlebach ends in Steinhaus, at the exit of the wild ravine of the Rüfi stream. In the Ärner forest, directly above the village on the path to the Frid mountain pasture, there's a pretty chapel at about 1500m (Jungfrau Maria), a once frequently visited place of pilgrimage since the 17th century; carefully restored in 1962 in its old style. Tennis, indoor pool. Group accommodation. Extensive walking country. Tourist information 3995 Ernen, tel: 027/9711562.

Binn (Schmidigehischere), 1400m

Binn is not the name of one individual village, the valley area consists of several hamlets: the main village Binn, originally called Schmidigehischere, Wilere (with the parish church), Heiligkreuz/Lengtal in the Leng valley, Ze Binne (at the confluence of the Binn and Leng valleys, reservoir), Giesse and Imfeld (Fäld), and Ausserbinn, halfway along from Ernen, on the sunny slope above the lower Binna gorge. Elegant arched bridge in Binn (1564) over the Binna, next to it the baroque Antonius chapel. Binn was the first community in Switzerland not to allow buildings of more than one storey in keeping with the nature of the region and in doing so encouraged the development of an area of nature preservation. Museum of local culture. Mineral collection. Campsite. The Binn valley is way above a »mineral treasure trove«, no where else in Switzerland are there comparably rich and exclusive crystal deposits, and a series of minerals was found exclusively here. In earlier times the search for crystals was commercially driven, but today you can try your luck in the waste pile in the Lengenbach cave. Especially rich diversity of plant species. Tourist information 3996 Binn, tel: 027/9714547.

Grengiols, 995m
Situated south of the Rotten in a hollow. Away from the main road it has remained wonderfully peaceful with its beautiful wooden houses and steep alleyways. In the war with the French the place was burnt down completely, but the fertility of the area enabled the inhabitants to rebuild. Incredible display of flowers in the meadows in early summer. Several small hamlets belong to Grengiols, such as Bächerhyschere (above), Bister (on the meadow terrace in the direction of Brig), Dreisch (on the other side of the Rotten on the valley road) or Hockmatte (opposite Außerbinn).
Tourist information 3993 Grengiols, tel:027/9271048.

Lax, 1039m
Small village on the Furka road below Fiesch on a meadow terrace. Ernen/Binntal turn offs on the other side of the Rotten and also to Martisberg. Tourist information 3994 Lax (with Martisberg), tel: 027/9711571.

Martisberg, 1348m – Betten, 1200m – Goppisberg, 1355m – Greich, 1361m – Ried ob Mörel, 1160 – 1340m
These small settlements lie about half way up the sunny slope of the mountain pasture ridge Riederhorn – Eggishorn. They have remained beautiful, quiet holiday places since the traffic rolls along the Rotten valley way below. However the big tourist attraction of the area is to be found much further up on the Riederalp and Bettmeralp and on Eggishorn – only Ried and Greich have been added as mid-way stations for the cable-cars to Riederalp. Marvellous walking country through cultivated landscape. Individual houses – of blackish-brown larch wood, of course – date back to the 15th century.

Bettmeralp, 1957m – Riederalp, 1925m
These former alpine meadow settlements on the sunny side of the ridge between the Rhône valley and the Aletsch glacier have developed into very pleasant resorts for sport and convalescence. Cars are not allowed but they are easily reached by several cable-cars from the FO stations. The Bettmeralp Maria zum Schnee chapel is particularly beautiful.
The region has been heavily developed for skiing, but offers many walks with stunning views, as in the Aletsch forest which is under environmental protection (Riederfurka environmental centre, Villa Cassel) or along the Aletsch glacier.
Mountain guide office, tennis, sports' centre with swimming pool, golf and minigolf, fishing and rowing on the Bettmer lake. Guided walks in the Aletsch forest and through the Massa gorge. Alpine meadow museum with displays, sunrise trips to the Bettmer ridge. Bunk houses, group accommodation.
Tourist information 3992 Bettmeralp, tel: 027/9271291 and 3987 Riederalp, tel: 027/9271365.

The Mischabel mountains from the path to Almagelleralp (Walk 26).

Mörel, 759m – Breiten, 864m

Mörel on the Rotten has a village centre worth visiting, with a parish church from the 13th century. Cable-car to the Tunetschalp, beautiful walking territory below the wild north cirques of Fülhorn and Bättlihorn. Breiten was first built in 1966, as a spa and health resort, with various sports on offer, tennis, solar-heated indoor pool. Tourist information 3983 Mörel, tel: 027/9271002.

Bitsch, 690 – 940m

At the mouth of the Massa gorge. Turn-off to Ried ob Mörel along a small road, chalets for visitors and flats for commuters to Brig. Massa electricity works. Tourist information 3982 Bitsch, tel: 027/9271784.

Blatten, 1327m

In a beautifully sunny and panoramic position in the Aletsch region above Brig/Naters. Well-preserved old houses and barns, one of the oldest settlements of the Valais (mentioned in 1079). Theoduls chapel from the 15th century, valley resort for the sunny Belalp terrace (cable-car). The chalet village of Tschuggen has been developed on the slope a little above. Tennis, squash, minigolf, bowling alleys, indoor pool. Group accommodation. Tourist information 3914 Blatten-Naters, tel: 027/9231385.

Belalp

Mountain pasture plateau above Blatten (cable-car). Brilliant view of the Aletsch glacier – best from the ridge at the Belalp hotel. Old village »Bäll« with chapel. Ski lift as far as the Hohstock. Horse riding (pony trekking), guided walks (across the Aletsch glacier to the Riederalp), St. Jakob's feast, Schäfersonntag (shepherds' Sunday). Group accommodation.

Naters, 673m

Until 1517 the main town of the Zehnden (= district), then Brig-Glis took over the honour. Church from the 17th c. (St. Mauritius) with tower (12th c.), restored priest house (parts 12/13th c.). For leisure activities, see Brig.

Brig, 684m

Together with Glis, the »capital« of the Upper Valais at the intersection of the rail and roads from the Lötschberg, Furka pass, Simplon pass and through the Rhône valley, also centrally placed as a base for all activities in the eastern Valais. Interesting, lively old town with shops and street cafés – after the catastrophic flood in the autumn of 1992 the whole centre was newly built, the pedestrian area was greatly extended. Brig profited especially in the 17th century from the activities of the businessman Kaspar Stockalper, who encouraged traffic over the Simplon pass. The Stockalper castle, the biggest palace in Switzerland is known far and wide, (17th century), also worth seeing the Kollegium and its church (1675 – 1685), as well as the parish church in Glis. Tennis, squash, swimming pools and thermal baths in Brigerbad, minigolf and cinema. Camping, group accommodation. Numerous walking possibilities in the surrounding area, varied programme of organised trips. The »Stockalper path« from Brig over the Simplon pass was restored with great dedication and in 1994 officially opened, as a kind of open-air museum – a path with evidence of former resting places, with stables or accomodation. Tourist information 3900 Brig, tel:027/9231901.

Termen, 920m – Ried ob Brig, 918m

Lovely villages on the open meadows to the west above Brig on the old Simplon road (a little way from the new fast road). Old village centres.

Rosswald, 1800 – 1960m

Especially sunny and panoramic village on the ridge above the Ganter valley and the Simplon road. Small access road from the old Simplon road, as well as a cable-car from above Ried. Small area of ski lifts on the ridge to the Folluhorn. Group accommodation. Tourist information Brig.

Rothwald, about 1850m – Wase, 1960m

Former alpine settlement, today mostly holiday chalets, ski lift to the Bodmertälli. Starting point for walks in the northern part of the Simplon area.

Simplon village, 1476m

A village that is still quiet, situated on the Simplon south ramp, with southern character. Border with Italy further down the valley in Gondo before the famous Gondo gorge. The Simplon pass has been, from time immemorial, an important crossing point of the Alps used by Romans (pack horse trails, 3rd century), Johanniter (hospice, 1235), Stockalper (path construction, hospice, 17th century) and Napoleon (military road, 1800 – 1805). In the last few years the »Stockalper path« has been restored and provides a journey back in time to the Middle Ages. A museum about the path is being built at present in a former inn. Eggen, the village lying above, shows the modest reconstruction of a once heavily populated village near to the present-day Homatta, which in 1597 was completely destroyed by an ice fall from the Homatta glacier. Below Simplon village lies Gstein-Gabi. Marvellous district for walking and mountain tours, surprisingly little known. Group accommodation. Tourist information 3901 Simplon, tel: 027/9791221.

Gondo, 855m – Zwischbergen, 1356m

Gondo is the Switzerland/Italy border station at the exit of the Gondo gorge. Narrow road from Gondo to Zwischbergen. Unfortunately the stream, the »Grosse Wasser« (= big water), has been reduced to a trickle by upstream energy production. The upper valley area, however, has lost hardly any of its beauty despite the constant building of new water management systems and alpine meadow roads. Former gold mining, at the start of the Zwischberg valley, stopped years ago due to lack of profit, in spite of many new attempts.

Birgisch, 1093m – Mund, 1190m

Birgisch is a small settlement above the Rhöne valley on the road to Mund. Mountain pastures with wonderful views on the sunny slopes above the village. Mund is situated on the other side of the Gredetsch valley, in the modern church there are the baroque altars worth seeing from the former church. Mund is the only place in Switzerland where saffron is grown commercially, in flower from the end of October to the beginning of November. Roadway to the settlement of Chastler.

Gamsen, 665 – Eyholz, 650m – Brigerbad, 655m – Lalden, 649m

The healing springs of Brigerbad have been well-known since the Middle Ages. During the course of centuries they have had fluctuating economic importance. Today there's a modern swimming pool and a curative bath, and a campsite. In Lalden there's an old village centre next to modern blocks of flats, agricultural holdings. Gamsen and Eyholz lie on the major road from Brig to Visp, there's heavy industrial development here. Tourist information 3900 Brigerbad, tel: 027/9464688.

Visp, 651m

At the confluence of the Vispa valley (Matter and Saas valleys) and the Rhône valley. Station of the SBB (Rhône valley) and the BVZ (to Zermatt), post bus station, thereby making practically all destinations in the eastern Valais easily accessible. Particularly interesting old town with winding alleys and historical buildings (partly from the 12th century) and utterly southern character. Increasing amount of bustling activity, in the evenings too, with street cafés and music. In the cultural centre »La Poste« there are dance and drama performances, concerts and other events, also of an international character. The second face of Visp is the Lonza works, a big chemical firm and the most important employer in the whole of the eastern Valais – complaints have been made for a long time from here about the noise pollution and smells and were, at one time, quite justified, but in the last few years there has been significant improvement. Dry and sunny climate, occasionally really hot in summer, but seldom humid. Several campsites, with open air pool, tennis, horse riding and other sporting activities. Numerous possibilities for trips into the surrounding area. Tourist information »Rund um Visp«, 3930 Visp, tel: 027/9466161.

Visperterminen, 1340m

Mountain village in marvellous sunny and panoramic position high above the Visp valley. Interesting old village centre with narrow, winding alleyways and paths between houses built in the typical Valais style. The wood from the here ever-present larch trees – dyed almost blackish-brown over the course of centuries – is the dominant building material. Modern parish church with Baroque altars. Kapellenweg to the forest chapel via the village of »Maria im Wald« with an organ dating from 1619. Visperterminen can boast (together with Zeneggen) that it is the community with the highest vineyard in Europe (up to 1100 metres).

The water was once conducted through long channels out of the Nanz valley round the ridge of the Gebidum, today however this is done through a tunnel in the mountain. Wonderful walking opportunities along the old channels, only recently restored in places. Group accommodation. Tourist information 3931 Visperterminen, tel: 027/9468060.

The delightfully situated Zmutt with a view of the Strahlhorn and Rimpfischhorn (Walk 35).

Zeneggen, 1374m

Zeneggen has an ancient history which goes back into the Bronze Age (chronicle from the year 1982 »Kleine Wunderwelt Zeneggen«). Chapel »Unner dem Biel« on a hill above the town. Excellent corn was cultivated for centuries on the terraces of the Zeneggen fields, providing seed corn for many regions in Switzerland. Vineyards up to 1100m. From 1937 to 1941 the then mayor, J. Kenzelmann, built the now famous Augstborderi water channel .

Bürchen, 1200 – 1650m – Unterbäch, 1180 – 1300m – Eischoll, 1219m

Bürchen is a community of small scattered settlements. Together with the neighbouring communities of Unterbäch and Eischoll, the fertile land of the terraces here below the Ginals valley was once cultivated. Pretty starting points for lovely panoramic walks on the meadows covered in flowers, particularly in early summer high above the Rhône valley. The ski lifts of the Augstbord region already reach far into the Ginals valley. Connection with the Törbel region via Moosalp. Tennis. Tourist information 3935 Bürchen, tel: 027/9341716, 3944 Unterbâch, tel: 027/9341085.

Stalden, 800m

Small village on a rocky hill above the confluence of the Saas and Matter Vispa. Old village centre with new Baroque parish church (high altar from the old church of Hérémence). The village is also known for the 14 bridges over the Vispa gorges, in places very old constructions. Station for the Visp-Zermatt line, roads into the Saas valley and the Matter valley as far as Täsch, also via Törbel to Moosalp and on the opposite side to Staldenried. You can also go there by cable-car which continues to Gspon where cars are not allowed. Tourist information 3922 Stalden, tel: 027/9521512.

Staldenried, about 1100m – Gspon, 1893m

Road and small cable-car from Stalden to Staldenried. Big, modern church. If you want to continue to the panoramic Gspon (chapel from 1694 with Baroque altar and huge crucifix) you can only go on foot or on the second section of the cable-car. This alpine settlement, where cars are not allowed, is the starting point for the famous Gspon ridge path to Saas Grund.

Grächen, 1619m

Famous holiday resort on the sunny terrace above the Matter valley, with big mountain panorama. Only since 1954 accessible on the road from St. Niklaus, before that the mule was the usual mode of transport along the steep mountain paths, today a beautiful walk. Village museum. Many kilometres of historic water channels which still today, if only partially with pipes, guarantees the watering of meadows and fields. Grächer forest (with Swiss pines and larch trees) above the village with many opportunities for walking. Seetalhorn and Hannigalp cable-cars. The demanding »Europa« path goes across the Matter valley to Täschalp (Grächen – Zermatt), information in the tourist offices. Tennis, squash, bowling, Vita Parcours, curling, minigolf, indoor pools and a children's adventure playground at Hannigalp, nature trail. Group accommodation. Tourist information 3925 Grächen, tel:027/9562727.

Saas Balen, 1483m

The lowest of the Saas communities, the round church from 1809 – 1812 is interesting, narrow, high Valais buildings, up to four storeys high (residential blocks with a separate house at the back). In nearby Bidermatten beautiful wooden houses and barns. High above Saas Balen there's the settlement of Heimischgarten, 2110m, with small chapel. Tourist information 3908 Saas Balen, tel: 027/9571689.

Saas Grund, 1559m

Main village in the Saas valley, before the tourist discovery of Saas Fee, also its economic centre. Trinity church with high altar from 1689 and historic organ of 1806. Wonderful walking country, but also starting point for high alpine activities. A good base for all activities in the Saas valley due to its central location. Cable-car via Kreuzboden to Hohsaas on the edge of the glacier under the Weißmies. Mountaineering school, sport centre with tennis, indoor pool. Group accomodation and several campsites. Tourist information 3910 Saas Grund, tel: 027/9572403.

Saas Almagell, 1672

The holiday resort which has remained the quietest of all the Saas communities. Simple ski lifts to Furggstalden. Group accommodation. Great walking country in meadows full of flowers and larch trees right up into the high mountain region. Guided tours of the power station (Mattmark reservoir). Tourist information 3905 Saas Almagell, tel: 027/9571653.

Saas Fee, 1790m

Picturesque mountain village surrounded by famous 4-thousanders which tower up out of the huge glaciers. Modern holiday resort with all that it entails, and yet still reasonably small. The village does not allow cars, but has cable-cars in three directions (Plattjen, Mittelallalin, Felskinn and Hannig), at times into rugged glacier country. Group accommodation, camping. Leisure centre with tennis, indoor pool, sauna, mountaineering school with a large programme of climbing trips, varied events for visitors. Saas museum with village history and minerals. Pay car parks at the entrance to the village (also a multi-storey car park), frequent post bus service from Visp. The access road has only been in existence since 1951, previously the pretty Kapellenweg from Saas Grund was the striking »entrée« into the glacier village for visitors. Great opportunities for excursions and walks directly out of the village, but on nearly all of them you come into contact with the mountain railways as well. Of course it saves you some effort on the ascent, but if you are really looking for peace and quiet you will have to walk a bit further. The views down into the valley basin are out of this world. From 1949 to 1978 the German poet and dramatist Carl Zuckmayer lived in the glacier village. He is also buried there. Tourist information 3906 Saas Fee, tel: 027/9571457.

Zermatt, 1616m

World famous tourist and mountaineering centre of the Valais Alps. The Matterhorn, without doubt, in the circle of the surrounding 4-thousanders, takes special place as a landmark of Zermatt (and the whole of Switzerland). Cars are not allowed, very good connections with Täsch (pay car parks). Youth hostel, group accommodation, campsite. Tennis courts, squash, indoor pools with sauna, curling, bowling alleys, minigolf and Vita Parcours. Mountain guide office with large choice of guided walks and mountain excursions. Place for numerous SAC huts, mountain bike paths, Gletschergarten (glacier garden) at the Gorner glacier outlet, paragliding. In Bahnhofstrasse there's often a frightening crush of people, but you can still find beautiful houses and quieter spots in some of the nearby alleyways. Alpine museum, art galleries, electric bus. Mountain railways to Unterrothorn, Gorner ridge and little Matterhorn/Schwarz lake. Many of the walks would be quieter if the railways were not there, but considerably more strenuous, and at least you can contemplate the day's experiences at night in the comfort of the valley. In any case you will still need to sacrifice a few drops of sweat in the name of mountain adventure. Tourist information 3920 Zermatt, tel: 027/9670181.

Täsch, 1450m
Unfortunately most Valais travellers treat Täsch only as a changeover point from the car to BVZ to Zermatt. This village is, however, worth a visit, situated at the end of the road with car parks for visitors to Zermatt. Village centre with rows of old houses, pretty church with tower from the 15th c., opportunities for hiking into the surrounding mountain landscape and the Zermatt area. Indoor pool. Campsite. Tourist information 3929 Täsch, tel: 027/9671689.

Randa, 1407m
Small village at the foot of the Weißhorn and Dom with old, sun-weathered wooden houses, church from 1726. Good base for a holiday in the Matter valley, where it should be much quieter than in the more famous Zermatt. Good connections (BVZ station). Campsite, group accommodation. Tourist information 3928 Randa, tel: 027/9671677.

St. Niklaus, 1116m – Mattsand, 1227m – Herbriggen, 1263m
Situated in the middle of the Matter valley, St. Niklaus was once the main village of this valley, but it has been struck several times by natural catastrophes. After an earlier tourist boom St. Niklaus could not survive the building of railways and roads to Zermatt. Only recently has there been economic change with the Scintilla AG (Bosch) factory with over 3000 employees, unusual for an alpine village. There has been a renewed upsurge in tourist development again. Interesting walking area. Station of the Brig-Visp-Zermatt railway. Junction with the road to Grächen, cable-car to the Jungu alpine settlement. Tennis and sports grounds, indoor pool, Vita Parcours. Tourist information 3924 St. Niklaus, tel: 027/9563663.

Törbel, 1497m – Embd, 1240 – 1450m
Both villages lie to the west on the flanks high above the Vispa valley near Stalden, many Valais houses still in their original style and barns. A lot of

Autumn walk on the Lötschberg south ramp (Walk 22).

work was put into the completion of an open-air museum in Törbel. On the round walk »Urchigs Terbil«, once common traditional buildings like a 300 year old barn, bake house, mill and other sights can be found. Embd may be the steepest village in the Alps, from the upper street it is at least 150m to the lower houses at the precipice into the Matter valley. Perfect walking country with stunning views, Road (post bus route) via Moosalp to Bürchen/Zeneggen. Small cable railway from Kalpetran to Embd. Tourist information 3923 Törbel, tel: 027/9522227.

Eggerberg, 843 – Außerberg, 1008m
Baltschieder, 645m – Hohtenn, 817m
Sunny villages in the area of the Lötschberg south ramp, the BLS from Brig to Goppenstein which ascends at the Lötschberg tunnel with wonderfully ingenious man-made construction and splendid views of the Valais Alps. Good roads from the Rhône valley, post bus connection with Visp. The aridity on these big south slopes made it necessary to build water channels out of the gorge-like side valleys (Baltschieder, Bietsch and Joli valleys) and sometimes in bold locations. Perfect walking country. A wild flower trail along the stream and a herb nature trail have recently been completed.

St. German, 757m – Raron, 638m
Turtig, 635m – Niedergesteln, 639m
Small villages in and a little above the Rhône valley west of Visp. In St. German above the vineyards there's a crypt in the restored village church from 1250. On the Heidnischbiel on the way to Raron is the St. Anna chapel where graves from the Bronze Age were found. Raron at the mouth of the Bietsch stream is an impressive village with old houses, the famous modern church (1972/74) is on the hill below the old church which was a castle until 1512. Museum in the castle (about people linked with the village, pro Raronia Historica foundation). At the church you will find the grave of Rainer Maria Rilke. Turtig is on the other side of the Rhône, cable-cars to the Eischoll and Unterbach villages of the Augstbord region. Niedergesteln also has an interesting village centre which is at the foot of the castle ruins. Wide areas of the Valais were ruled from here in the 12th century. Campsites. Tourist information 3942 Raron, tel: 027/9343100.

Gampel-Steg, 635m
Villages at the end of the Lötschen valley, left and right of the Lonza. Villages with southern character, industry (Alusuisse in the middle of the fields in the east), former purification works of the Goppenstein lead mine. Road to the Lötschberg car loading for Goppenstein. Cable-car to Jeizinen (»Leuker Sonnenberge« region). Indoor pool, campsites. Tourist information 3945 Gampel-Bratsch, tel: 027/9322460.

Goppenstein, 1216m

Loading station for the Lötscgberg tunnel with very busy commuter traffic to Kandersteg on the Bernese side. Former sites of the lead mine companies which, with few exceptions, mined lead and silver here with little success. The veins carrying ore were too marginal in production, the land too hard to work. Station for the bus into the Lötschen valley.

Ferden, 13755m – Kippel, 1376m – Wiler, 1419m

Small villages in the still wonderfully quiet Lötschen valley with magnificent opportunities for walking at the foot of the Bietschhorn and Peters ridge. Cable-car from Wiler to Lauchernalp (Lötschen valley ridge path). The Lötschen pass from Ferden into the Gastere valley (Kandersteg) has historic significance. All the villages in the Lötschen valley are worth a visit, Lötschen valley museum in Kippel (ore mining, minerals, local information). Well-known customs: carnival procession, Herrgottgrenadiere. Tennis, bunk house, campsite (in Kippel). Lötschen valley tourist information 3918 Wiler, tel: 027/9391388,

Blatten, 1540m

Highest village in the Lötschen valley, the road continues to Fafleralp. Compact village, many old houses. Great walking area.

Turtmann, 630m – Niedergampel, 648m – Getwing, 626m

Turtmann is the village at the mouth of the Turtmann valley into the Rhône valley, predominantly agricultural trade. On the dry slope above Getwing you will find a botanical rarity, the Perückenstrauch, in abundance. The whole slope turns unbelievably red in autumn. Tourist information 3951 Turtmann, tel: 027/9321691.

Ergisch, 1085m – Unterems, 1003m – Oberems, 1332m

Small villages on both sides above the end of the Turtmann valley, very beautiful villages with many old houses. Attractive walking country into the quiet Turtmann valley and the areas of Eischoll – Unterbäch as well as Meretschialp. The Turtmann valley road connects Unterems and Oberems with Turtmann in the Rhône valley, also cable-car connection. Ergisch can be reached along a narrow road. Tourist information 3948 Oberems, tel: 027/9321000.

Gruben-Meiden, 1822m

Small summer settlement in the Turtmann village, extensive and peaceful walking country, village of the Turtmann hut, stopover on the connecting walking route from the Zinal to the Matter valley. Chapel from 1708, inn with tourist accommodation.

Agarn, 626m – Susten, 630m
Two villages in the Leuker ground, in the catchment area of the wild Illgraben, the Dala gorge (of Leukerbad) and the hidden Feschel gorge. You will find nearby the Pfyn forest, the only unspoilt area on the Rhône. Campsites.

Leuk, 731m – Inden, 1138m
Leuk lies a little above the confluence of the Leuker stream (Dala gorge) into the Rhône valley near large vineyards, historic centre (bishops' castle for 1150, Ringacker chapel (1694), town hall from the 13th century, parish church with tower 11th century). Museum of local culture, indoor and open-air pools, tennis, horse riding. Campsites in the area. Just above at Brentjong there's a satellite ground station (visitor centre). Inden is a small village on the road to Leuk via the Dala gorge. Tourist information 3952 Leuk (with Susten), tel: 027/4731094.

Albinen, 1274m – Guttet, 1345m – Feschel, 1280m
Erschmatt, 1228m – Bratsch, 1103m – Jeizinen, 1526m
These small villages are brought together in the region »Leuker Sonnenberge«. Small roads connect the villages with Leuk and via Albinen with Leukerbad. Walking country with superlative views: the show case of the Valais Alps are lined up in the south directly opposite the sharp pyramid of the Weißhorn. There's only a small ski-lift near Jeizinen, otherwise this is perfect countryside for walkers, with pretty villages and sun-weathered houses made of larch wood. Tourist information 3941 Albinen, tel: 027/4734391, 3956 Feschel-Guttet, tel: 027/4731367.

Leukerbad, 1402m
Spa with thermal springs, famous far beyond the Valais border, situated amidst wonderful scenery below the Gemmi pass (historic mountain path and cable-car). Wide range of sports on offer, and not only the usual ones for alpine villages: athletics, football, tennis, squash … Extensive walking area. Cable-cars up to Gemmi (crossing into Kander valley) and to Torrent with beautiful ridge paths (at the weekend direct buses between Leukerbad and Goppenstein, interesting for the ridge paths between both valleys and into the Bernese Oberland). Group accommodation, camping. Less pleasing are the plans for building more lifts on the delightful slopes of the Torrent in the direction of Albinen (Leuker Sonnenberge). Tourist information 3954 Leukerbad, tel: 027/4727171.

Varen (Varone), 760m – Salgesch, 581m
Two wine villages near the language boundary. Vine and wine museum, vineyard path (Sentier viticole) Salgesch – Sierre with 45 information boards about wine growing and pressing. Nature conservation area in the Raspille

Above Leukerbad the clouds slide over the Gemmi pass like a waterfall.

gorge. A rock fall in the Ice Age from the Varneralp onto the Rhône glacier, which at that time covered the Rhône valley, is today deposited in the hills of the Plyn forest.

Old bridge with bridge tower over the Dala between Varen and Leuk, until 1990 the only approach road from there to Varen. Today there is a new bridge over the Dala gorge. Tennis courts, campsite. Office du tourisme 3960 Sierre, tel: 027/4558535.

Tips for rainy days and rest days

The following is – without claiming to be complete – a short review of the most important attractions in the whole of the Valais and will hopefully make easier the choice of activities, that do not include going to a summit.

Thermal baths in Mörel, Brigerbad, Leukerbad, Saillon les Bains, Val d'Illiez and Lavey les Bains.

Wild river rafting in the Upper Goms.

Underground lakes and caves in St. Léonard (Lac Souterrain), Anzère (Rawil) and St. Maurice (Grotte aux Fées).

Glacier ice caves on the Furka pass (Rhône glacier) and in Saas Fee (Fee glacier).

Gorges at Brig (Massa), on the Simplon pass (Gondo), at Susten/Agarn (Illgraben and Feschelklamm), in the Val d'Anniviers (at Pontis), at Sion (Lizerne gorge) and at Martigny (Gorges du Dumand and Gorges du Trient).

Waterfalls at Rèchy and at Martigny (Pissevache).

Gletschergarten (glacier garden) in Zermatt.

Earth pyramids at Euseigne.

Reservoirs of Mattmark, Moiry, Dixence, Mauvoisin and Emosson.

Mineral collections/geological exhibitions on the Grimsel pass, in Binn, Kippel (Biel mine), Zinal (copper mine), Les Haudères and on the Col de Montets.

Botanic gardens in Champex and Bourg Saint Pierre as well as on the Col des Montets.

Alpine zoo in Les Marécottes.

Museums: in the last few years many villages have built museums of local culture with expertise and attention to detail – they are not dusty piles of junk from the past, but highly interesting collections and lavishly restored tools, houses or barns. In this region of extremes, especially in the once isolated side valleys, there's now a healthy respect for the achievements of earlier generations. Only a limited selection can be mentioned here: Binn, Brig, Kippel, Eggerberg, Saas Fee, Törbel, Sion, Praz-de-Fort.

Alpine meadow museums (cheese making exhibitions) and alpine meadow guided tours in Riederalp/Bettmeralp, Nax, Ovronnaz.

Alpine museums in Zermatt, Bern and Chamonix

Archaeolgical museum in Martigny.

Natural history museum in Sion.

A train of the Furka Oberalp railway near Grengiols (Walk 8).

Wine museum in Sierre. Wine cellar visits with wine-tasting and sales in most
of the wine areas.
Car museum in Martigny.

Added to this many villages organise events (concerts, lectures, excursions),
also open-air plays and festivals. There are all sorts of village festivals,
processions, mountain guide festivals, alpine meadow parades and shepherds' feasts. Also to be mentioned is cow fighting, bloodless cow fights
attended by folk festival characters. The strongest cow becomes queen – a
title connected with honour and prizes, first for the animal receiving her stall
and meadow comrades' respect, and then for the owner.

Also recommended, due to the excellent transport connections, are trips into
neighbouring countries or cantons:
– via the Nufenen pass into the Tessin (post bus).
– under the Furka pass to Andermatt (Furka Oberalp railway)
– over the Grimsel pass to Meiringen and to the Brienzer lake (post bus)
– through the Lötschberg to the Thuner lake and to Bern (BLS railway)
– over the Simplon pass to Domodossola, to the Lago Maggiore and Lago
  d'Orta (BLS railway in the tunnel, post bus via the pass)
– over the Grand Saint Bernard (or through it) to Aosta (MO bus)
– over the Col de la Forclaz/Montets to Chamonix (MC railway)
– to Genf lake (SBB).

Important telephone numbers

Swiss tourist office:	
All over Europe you can use the following numbers	
tel:	0080010020030
fax:	0080010020031
Valais Tourist Information, Sion:	027/3273570
Weather report:	0041/1/162
Internet:	www.Myswitzerland.com

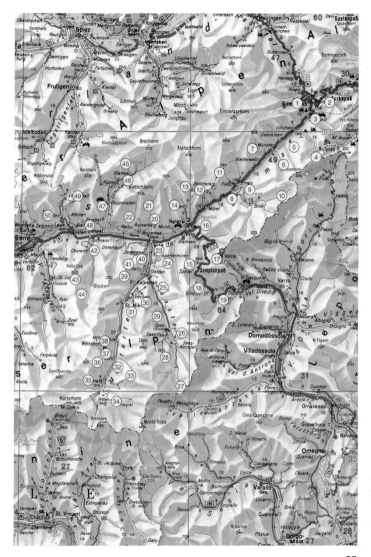

1 Sidelhorn, 2764m

With little exertion up to a high view point

Grimsel pass – Husegg hut – Sidelhorn

Location : Gletsch, 1757m. Bus connection with Oberwald (FO station).
Starting point: Grimsel pass, 2165m, popular crossing point over the pass from central Switzerland into the Valais, only open in summer. Particularly impressive landscape on the drive up from the north with rock faces of compact granite similar to those in Yosemite – a sport climber's paradise. Bus to the pass (4 times a day, 25 min from Oberwald, 18km). Parking on the pass.
Walking times: climb to the summit 1¾ hrs, descent 1¼ hrs.
Ascent: 600m.
Grade: easy walk, on good paths as far as the last swing up to the summit, the last section is a marked path through a boulder field.
Stops and accommodation: restaurants at the top of the pass (open in summer), hotel and mass accomodation.
Worth seeing: Totensee (lake of the dead), deep blue lake at the top of the pass. Large

reservoirs on the north ramp. Mineral and crystal room with shop. Extensive view of the Rhône glacier and the highest peaks of the Bernese Alps.

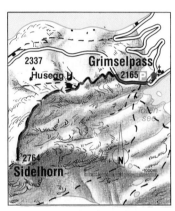

The **Grimsel pass** is one of Switzerland's most spectacular mountain passes, so you should expect it to be very busy in high summer especially at weekends. You can drive northward, as far as the Oberaar lake along the road to the power station below the Sidelhorn.

Ascent to the Sidelhorn: at the car parks on the big bend at the top of the pass the road to the power station branches off westwards to the Oberaar lake. Follow this for only about 500m to just before a cable-car station for the power station traffic. A signpost indicates the path which zigzags up between the polished round granite humps – an alpine playground not only for children – onto the ridge to the **Husegg hut** (closed). Despite a signpost, do not turn off before, it's only a shortcut. With beautiful views continue along the ridge which, gently curving round to the left, brings you to the boulder summit. You reach the highest point along a path winding up the short, steepish flank.

The **return** to the pass is back along the same route.

The Grimsel pass with the Totensee, and Sidelhorn above.

2 Groß Muttenhorn, 3099m

High summit in the upper Valais with an alpine feel

Furka pass – Mutt glacier – Tällistock – Groß Muttenhorn

Location: Gletsch, 1757m, summer settlement, in the upper area under the rapidly retreating Rhône glacier. Intersection of the Furka and Grimsel pass roads. Post bus connection with Oberwald (about 4 buses a day, 9km, 10 minute journey).

Starting point: Furka pass, 2431m, one of the highest road passes in Switzerland. Post bus connection over the pass to Andermatt (from Gletsch to the top of the pass 15km, a good 25 minute journey).

Walking times: Furka pass – Mutt glacier 45 minutes, ascent of Tällistock 1 hr, ridge crossing to the Muttenhorn 1¼ hrs, return 2 hrs.

Ascent: 700m.

Grade: easy mountain walk as far as the Tällistock, then sometimes only traces of a narrow path, after the pre-summit a few metres of easy scrambling (a good head for heights and sure-footedness needed here).

Stops and accommodation: restaurant on the Furka pass (east side) and at Belvedere (west side on the Rhône glacier). No facilities on the way.

Worth seeing: very beautiful flora in summer on the way to the glacier, Tällistock already offers open views of the Valais and Bernese Alps, on the Groß Muttenhorn the panorama extends to the silent mountains of the Rotondo range. The north is dominated by the Galenstock above the Rhône glacier.

From the top of the **Furka pass** go along the military road to the south (signpost) and high above the valley as far as the fields of debris under the **Mutt glacier**. Cross over the outlet and continue another 300m on the other side, then branch off left (signpost) and the path zigzags to a flat col north of the Tällistock. The secondary summit now rises up in the south and you go

On the Groß Muttenhorn with views of the Bernese Alps.

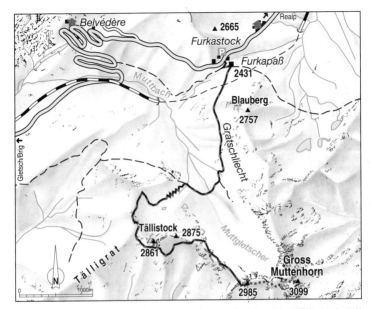

round this to the right (west) and reach the south side of the **Tällistock** and continue up in a few minutes to the summit.

The path to the **Groß Muttenhorn** crosses the south side of the Tällistock and reaches the connecting ridge after about 800m. The now narrow path continues along the ridge, partly through sparse vegetation and partly over fields of debris or rough boulders, until you reach the secondary summit without any great problems.

The ridge, hitherto quite broad, changes in character here and becomes rocky for a short way – only the experienced mountaineer should go any further. Indistinct tracks lead slightly to the right (south) of the edge for a short way down into the upper section of a scree gully. The rocks on the other side can be climbed over, but it's much easier to climb diagonally right up some terraces into a small rocky cleft where a boulder has split off from the rock.

You can then traverse on a band under the rocky ridge till you reach the end (sections of grade I). The final climb turns out to be quite unproblematic and zigzags over a scree ridge to the summit.

The **return** to the pass is back along the same route.

3 Gere valley

Walk into a spoilt paradise

Oberwald – Schärlichwang – Schweif – Oberwald

Location and starting point: Oberwald, 1368m, FO (Furka – Oberwald railway) station. Parking in the sparse larch wood, reached from the main road over the Rhône through the village area of Unterwassern.
Walking times: Oberwald – Schärlichwang 1½ hrs, Schärlichwang – Schweif 1 hr, return 2 hrs.

Ascent: 480m.
Highest point: about 1850m, above Schweif.
Grade: easy walk on clear paths without difficulty. No facilities on the way.
Worth seeing: Unterwassern village centre, Goneri gorge, Goneriwasser ravine. Climbing area with impressive granite rock faces.

The high valley of Gere was until the year 1986 totally unspoilt – the stream was still running, a rarity in the Valais with its many reservoirs. Walking into this dry valley you could imagine that you were in the pioneering times of alpinism. Under the pretext of building a mountain pasture road and business route the military department (EMD) began blasting a broad road into the valley, destroying nature, in order to erect a shooting range in the middle part. In many areas the Valais has been transformed by the overdevelopment of settlements, large reservoirs, re-routed streams and destroyed cultivation. One of the saddest examples is this road, originally an alpine meadow route transformed into a totally senseless shooting range.

Go up from the car park at **Oberwald** over the Goneri and along a narrow tarmac road above the Goneri gorge. Do not go up to Gere, but turn right 300m beforehand down into the valley bottom of the Gerenwasser. Continue winding up higher into the forest and eastwards into the **Gere valley**.

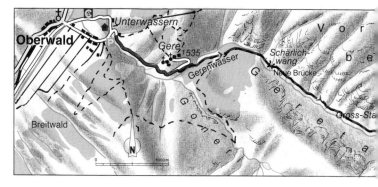

In the wild, romantic upper Gere valley.

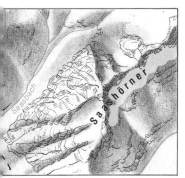

Go across the bridge at **Schär-lichwang** and along a beautiful narrow path on the east side of the stream through the valley to Groß Stafel and **Schweif**.

The wonderful Saas stream comes down from the northeast and joins the Gerenwasser. There's a great view of the small glaciers and the craggy ridges bordering the valley.

The **return** path is back along the same route.

4   Bättelmatthorn, 3044m

Little known 3-thousander – accessible to mountain walkers

Nufenen pass road – Gries pass – Bättelmatthorn

Location: Ulrichen, 1346m, FO station.
Starting point: Nufenen pass road, works road turn-off to the Gries pass, 2479m. Post bus stop (3 buses a day, 20 minute journey from Ulrichen, 15km). Parking on the works road.
Walking times: bus stop on the Nufenen pass road – Gries pass 1 hr, continuing to the Bättelmatthorn 2¼ hrs, return to the road 2¼ hrs.

Ascent: 770m.
Grade: alpine mountain walk on good paths as far as the Gries pass, only traces of a path on the upper section to the summit. Sure footedness needed here. No facilities on the way.
Worth seeing: the Gries glacier reaches almost down to the water when the Gries lake is dammed up. The landscape here exhibits almost arctic traits.

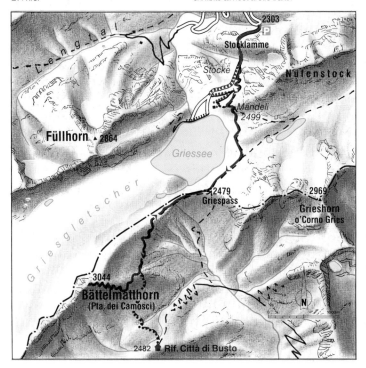

A few years ago the tongue of the Gries glacier still reached down into the water of the Gries lake. Bättelmann is on the left of the picture.

The Bättelmatthorn is an outstanding peak giving views to the north of the Bernese Alps with the striking Finsteraarhorn, and to the south of the Gries glacier with the Blinnenhorn and in the upper Valle del Gries with the Ofenhorn and the Sabbione reservoir. The path goes on Italian soil so do not forget your passport.

From the **Nufenen pass road** you go along the works road which ascends gently uphill round a ridge to the Stocklamme where steep avalanche valleys drop down to the valley floor. A shortcut leads off left here up to Mändeli, 2499m, from where there's a magnificent view of the Gries lake. You can also continue along the roadway and reach the same point which only takes a few minutes longer. About 100m high above the eastern shore of the lake there are short ups-and-downs over to the **Gries pass**, 2479m, and the border.

Ascent to the Bättelmatthorn: from the pass follow the path westwards on the northeast ridge of the Bättelmatthorn, which is still wide at this point, past the glacier chippings and fragments of moraine. At a height of about 2650m the path crosses onto the debris-covered eastern flank. Before descending once more to reach the Italian huts Citta di Busto and Mores a feint track branches off to the right which soon becomes more distinct and ascends diagonally upwards to the east ridge. Go onto the ridge at a tiny cleft. Keeping along the tracks on the left edge going north, you zigzag up to the summit of the **Bättelmatthorn**. Where the path is a little more distinct keep as close as possible to the edge.

The **descent** is back along the same path.

5 Brudelhorn, 2791m

Large viewing summit above the Goms

Nufenen pass road/Ladstafel – Vorderdistelalp – Distel lake – Brudelhorn

Location: Ulrichen, 1346m, beautiful village at the turn-off to the Nufenen pass from the Rhône valley, FO station.

Starting point: Ladstafel, 1925m, stopping point for the post bus to the Nufenen pass (about 3 buses a day, 25 minute journey Ulrichen – top of the pass) on the small Mässmatte plateau, before the road winds up to the top of the pass.

Walking times: Ladstafel – Vorderdistelalp 1½ hrs, continuation to the Distal lake 50 minutes, summit climb 40 minutes, about 3 hrs in total. Return 1¾ hrs.

Ascent: 870m.

Grade: mountain walk on good paths, altitude and length of walk require the relevant equipment and time planning.

Stops and accommodation: restaurants in Ulrichen and on the Nufenen pass. No facilities on the way.

Worth seeing: interesting flora in this desolate mountain region. The picturesque Distel lake lies in the uppermost region below the summit with a view of the rather glaciated ridge of the Ritzhörner as far as the Merezebachschije in the south. In the north there's a view over to the Bernese Alps, dominated by the Finsteraarhorn, and down to the valley floor of the Goms with its small villages.

From the **Ladstafel** bus stop go to the beautifully shaped old bridge over the Ägene stream and there climb diagonally up across the hillside covered in thin bushes to the cleft of the Leng valley with the alpine pasture of the same name. First in the valley bottom, then gently gaining height on the

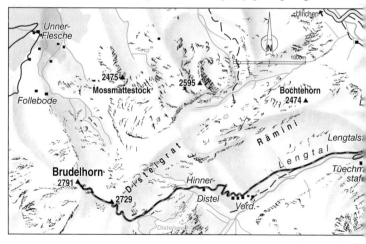

Münster in the Goms; the slopes on the right go up to the Brudelhorn.

northern meadow slopes, you reach the **Vorderdistelalp** situated on a small terrace – the back of the valley is dominated by scree gullies and snowfields. The path continues across the sunny meadows up to the right and into the interesting little Hinnerdistel high valley with water running

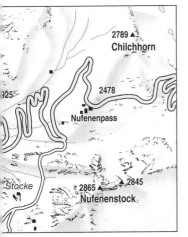

down from all sides, small bogs and in between piles of smoothly polished rock.

Keeping a little more to the left, going westwards, you soon come to the shores of the delightfully situated **Distel lake** – this spot could be your day's objective in its own right!

However, the path continues diagonally across the northern slope to the very broad Distel ridge, covered in debris, and then in a few minutes to the **Brudelhorn** a little way to the north.

On your **return** along the ascent path the afternoon light gives a totally different impression of the landscape.

6 Blinnen valley

Walk into a remote high valley

Reckingen – Lärch – Blinnen glacier

Location and starting point: Reckingen, 1326m, sizable village in the Goms with interesting sections of the village. FO station.
Walking times: Reckingen – Lärch 2 hrs, continuing to the Blinnen glacier 45 minutes, return to Reckingen 2 hrs.
Ascent: 720m.
Highest point: glacier apron, about 2050m.
Grade: easy walk, lengthy sections on broad forest track. No facilities on the way.

Worth seeing/alternative: the Blinnen valley is a natural valley, at the start lined with rocky slopes, then with very steep meadow slopes and eventually with debris below the Blinnenhorn. Fit mountain walkers can climb steeply up a narrow path from the furthest point in the valley to the Chummehorn (2 hrs and then 2½ – 3 hrs for the walk out through the Rappen valley to Mühlebach), a totally peaceful and remote experience!

From the station in **Reckingen** go across the quaint covered wooden bridge and through the settlement of Überrotte to the start of the **Blinnen valley**. At the no-entry sign a footpath continues straight upwards to the small chapel and meets the roadway again a little further up. Walk along this, gradually ascending, into the valley. From Salzgäbi the valley goes in an almost straight line towards the basin below the Blinnenhorn, but the glacier is still hidden from view. The last little wood is by the **Lärch** hut – as the name suggests, it is built almost exclusively of larch trees. The roadway soon comes to an end and a path continues further into the valley amidst amazing landscape, an open geology textbook! Sharply cut side streams, steep

Above the end of the Blinnen valley you can see the Galmihorn (Bernese Alps).

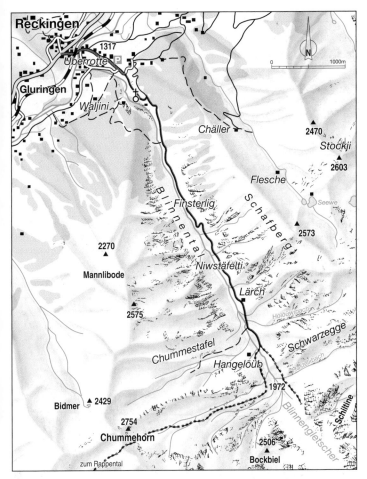

meadow slopes towering up and chaotic slopes of broken rock. In order to be able to see the complete **Blinnen glacier** you would still need to climb quite a way up its lower snowfields, but the surroundings are impressive enough down here.

The **return** is back the same way.

7 Gommer ridge path

High above the upper Rhône valley

Bellwald – Reckingen

Location: Fürgangen, 1120m, village above Fiesch on the FO (40 minutes from Brig, almost every hr) and on the road into the Goms. Parking at the station.

Starting point: Bellwald, 1559m. Ideally reached by cable railway from Fürgangen station. Once inside the cable-car, telephone the mountain station to get it started from there, and pay when you arrive (open between about 6.00 and 20.00).

Walking times: Bellwald – Bieliger valley 3 hrs, Bieliger valley – Reckingen stream 1 – 1½ hrs, descent to Reckingen 1 hr. Total time 5 – 5½ hrs.

Highest point: Reckingen stream, about 1800m.

Grade: easy, well marked walk.

Stops and accommodation: restaurants and inns in Bellwald and Reckingen. No facilities on the way.

Worth seeing: very informative view of the whole of the upper Goms area. In Reckingen market square opposite the church there's a memorial for the 30 people who died in the avalanche catastrophe on 24th February, 1970. This was the reason for building the enormous avalanche barriers to the west of the village.

You can walk the sunny Gommer ridge path well into late autumn.

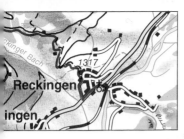

The Gommer ridge path – a trail made by the Goms communities – goes through the whole valley high up on its sunny southeast slopes. The complete walk goes from Bellwald to Oberwald in about 9 to 10 hrs.

From the cable-car station in **Bellwald** follow the signs eastwards round the village and uphill past beautiful barns. Following the sign to the right above Wilera, go across the hillside over fairly level meadows, over a stream and descend to the stream called »Schwarzer Brunnen« above the 1622m point. Continue down to the cluster of houses in Wiler, 1371m, above Blitzingen. Go left over a stream and zigzag up to the 1594m point. Right again through the forest, over Hilpersch stream and once more through the forest gently ascending into the cleft of the **Wali stream** with fine views of the Wasenhorn and the Vorderes Galmihorn.

On the other side of the stream alternating between forest and meadows continue on fairly level ground round a mountain ridge immediately followed by another. From this ridge there's a path leading down to the **Reckingen stream**. Descend easily on the lower path till a path turns off right to **Reckingen** which goes to the avalanche protection barrier. Eventually, in a few minutes, you reach the village and the train station.

Return to Fürgangen by FO train.

8 Grengiols – Binn valley

Peaceful walk from Grengiols into the Binn valley

Grengiols – Hockmatta – Steinmatten – Binn

Location and starting point: Grengiols, 995m, situated in the south on the meadow terrace above the Rotten as it flows through a deep ravine, FO station (the station lies about 100m below the village).
Destination: Binn (Schmidigehischere), 1400m, main village in the Binn valley, bus connection with Fiesch (about 9 buses a day, 30 minute journey from Binn to Fiesch, FO station); return to Grengiols from here by FO trains.
Walking times: Grengiols station – Grengiols 20 minutes, Grengiols – Hockmatta 1 hr, Hockmatta – Steinmatten 45 minutes,

Steinmatten – Binn 45 minutes. Total time 3 hrs.
Ascent: 600m.
Highest point: Binn, 1400m.
Grade: easy walk on broad paths.
Stops and accommodation: restaurants in Grengiols and Binn.
Worth seeing: the walk partly goes round the Breithorn massif which reveals strange, steep, sheer gullies. The rich splendour of the flowers invites you to linger, especially in early summer, and you would have difficulty in finding anything comparable. The Binna gorge is with you for a good part of the way.

From **Grengiols** station you go along the road up into the village. The centre is worth a visit – narrow steep alleyways, houses weathered by the wind and sun. A roadway now goes up over the meadows to the small hamlet of Bächerhyschere (Bächerhäusern). Continue gently uphill through the meadows to two gullies which drop down abruptly from the summit of the

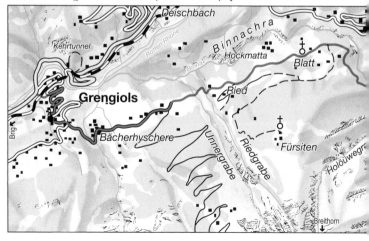

As if split with a giant axe – the Breithorn with its strange mountain gullies.

Breithorn. On a level path, alternately through forest and meadows, with views of the Binna gorge, past **Hockmatta** to the Blatt chapel. Here, above the bend of the Binna gorge, you enter the high forest where the path descends slowly into the valley bottom, crosses the Binna and on the other side leads round 2 bends to the **Steinmatten** houses on the road up to Binn. At this point the road disappears into a tunnel, about 1.5km long. You take,

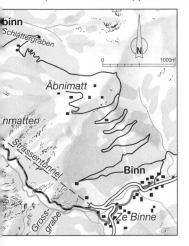

however, the old track which continues across the steep slope above the sharply indented valley. In some places it becomes clear that the tunnel is the only safe approach in winter – the old road, cut from horrendously steep, broken rocks, has been buried time and time again. On the slope opposite are two more sheer, deep gullies. Eventually you come to the small reservoir and walk along beside it, past the Ze Binne houses, to Binn.

Take the bus to Fiesch and continue by FO, a very interesting section (tunnel loops backwards at the steep section), back to Grengiols.

9 Eggerhorn, 2503m

Belvedere with beautiful views of the Bernese and Valais Alps

Ernen – Alpe Frid – Eggerhorn – Sattulti – Binn

Location: Ernen, 1195m, bus connection with Fiesch. Binn (Schmidigehischere), 1400m, bus connection with Fiesch via Ernen (about 2 buses a day, 30 minute journey, 14km). Parking in the village.

Starting point: Alpe Frid, end of the road at the pond, 1762m. A narrow tarmac road goes from Ernen to this idyllic little spot at the edge of the forest. Transfer by mini-bus from a local taxi firm (information from the tourist office), which saves about 1½ hrs on the ascent. If you decide not to descend to Binn and want to come back on the same path, you can drive up and park below Alpe Frid.

Walking times: pond – Alpe Frid 20 minutes, Alpe Frid – Eggerhorn 2 hrs, descent to Binn 2 hrs (back to Alpe Frid 1¼ hrs).
Ascent: 740m.
Grade: easy summit walk on good, but very steep paths. No facilities.
Worth seeing: the villages of Ernen and Binn. Magnificent larch trees at the edge of the forest, extensive views of most of the 4-thousanders of the Bernese Alps, as well as interesting, much less well-known views of the Leone mountains in the eastern Valais Alps.

Ascent to the Eggerhorn: from **Ernen** or from the car park at the water bassin go along the roadway to the nearby **Alpe Frid** and continue east-

Ernen is one of the most picturesque village in the Valais.

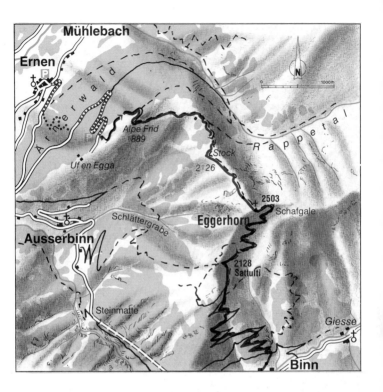

wards to a fork where a path goes straight on into the Rappen valley, but your path turns off right and leads through a thin wood of larch trees and eventually goes up steeply to the Stock. The views open out northwards to the Bernese Alps and you can see the silent Rappen valley in its entirety. A short level section follows and then the remaining steep climb. It's a fairly direct path to the **Eggerhorn** summit, deep and water-eroded, through an area of tiny bushes and alpine meadows. The northern summit has a cross on the top, the slightly higher southern summit forms a grassy hilltop.

Return to Binn: the good path meanders along the south side of the summit to the **Sattulti**, 2128m, and meets a roadway which winds down through a beautiful forest – a footpath cuts out some of the zigzags.

10 Binn valley hut – Albrun pass, 2409m

Switzerland's mineral paradise

Imfeld – Chiestafel – Binn valley hut – Albrun pass – Imfeld

Location and starting point: Imfeld (Fäld), 1519m, small settlement above the confluence of the Binna and the Fäldbach with picturesque old houses. Cars must be left in the pay car park before the Binna bridge. Post bus connection Fiesch – Binn (about 7 a day, 30 minute journey, 14km), taxi to Imfeld.

Walking times: Imfeld – Chiestafel 2¼ hrs, path to the Binntal hut 1 hr, ascent to the Albrun pass ½ hr. Total time about 3¾ hrs. Descent 2½ hrs. Valley path Binn – Imfeld 40 minutes.

Ascent: 950m.

Highest point: Albrun pass, 2409m.

Grade: good, sufficiently marked paths, roadway from Chiestafel on the return.

Stops and accommodation: the SAC Binntal hut is a »genuine« mountain hut and has not yet turned into a fast food restaurant. Drinks and simple catering from end of June to beginning of October. Recommended hut accommodation. »Imfeld« restaurant at the car park, open May to mid October.

Worth seeing: unique geological structure: wide variety of rock types and formations can be seen in a small area. Famous for its crystal and rich mineral resources. Diverse flora.

The Binn valley has been under environmental protection since 1964 – and is not yet overrun by mass tourism! Guided tours covering the geology and mineral resources of the area are available for those who are interested.

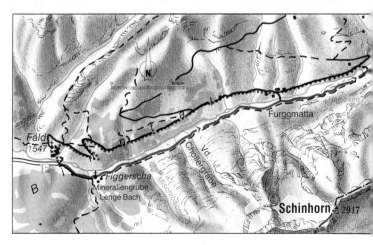

The Binn valley hut makes wonderful walking country.

From the Binna bridge below **Imfeld** follow the sign to the »Mineraliengrube«. At Figgerscha, however, do not go up to the mine at Lenge Bach, stay on the footpath which runs along the south side of the Binna into the valley and after Furggmatta, leads up to the picturesque Halse lake. Then in a few minutes you come down to the **Chiestafel** bridge where there's an area of striking, pure white dolomite.

The next stage of the good path goes on the north side of the little gorge to

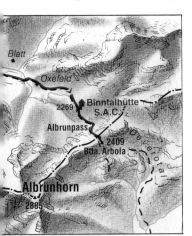

the plain of Blatt and reaches Oxefeld from where you ascend comfortably to the now visible **Binntal hut**. Continue in the same direction to the **Albrun pass**. The path goes round some bends to the lowest col – if you have enough time you should climb up to one of the hills on either side of the pass or go down a short way onto the Italian side where there's also a marvellous view into the Dévero valley, a real walkers' paradise.

Descent: return on the same path back to Chiestafel, but then take the track on the northern (right hand) side back to **Imfeld**. You can take a shortcut along a footpath across the last bends above the settlement.

11 Märjelen lake – Eggishorn, 2927m

Aletsch highlights with an Arctic feel

Bettmer ridge – Märjelen lake – Eggishorn

Location: Bettmeralp, 1957m, situated on a sunny terrace above Fiesch, no cars allowed but easily accessible by cable car (half hourly service between about 6.00 and 23.00) from Betten (station and car parks).

Starting point: Bettmer ridge, 2643m, mountain station of Bettmeralp cable railway.

Walking times: Bettmer ridge mountain station – Märjelen lake 1¼ hrs, Märjelen lake – Eggishorn mountain station 2½ hrs, detour to the Eggishorn ½ hr.

Ascent: 630m.

Grade: easy mountain walk.

Stops and accommodation: at the mountain station of the Bettmer ridge and Eggishorn cable cars (kiosk), Märjelen hut at Märjelen lake and Kühboden station.

Worth seeing: Märjelen lake on the Aletsch glacier, from which the ice dams up the meltwater. Beautiful lakes and interesting high moor biotope on Märjelenalp. Great views of the Aletsch glacier, especially from the Bettmerhorn and Eggishorn stations. Guided glacier walks (information at the tourist office in Bettmeralp).

Märjelen lake was once much larger and used to break regularly through the retaining ice wall, pouring along the glacier into the valley and causing severe destruction in the Brig area. Hydraulic engineering has put a stop to that and the lake is usually only in evidence when the snow is melting (photo on page 9).

Aletsch glacier path: from **Bettmer ridge mountain station** go a few metres, almost horizontally, round the Bettmerhorn ridge on its north side, where the newly-laid path leads just under the rocks diagonally northwards. With a magnificent view of the Aletsch glacier and the surrounding peaks you reach the Große Gufer.

Descend a short way until you reach the junction with the lower, old ridge path at Roti Chumma. The path – in places cut into the rocks – now leads across flat ground to the cut-off point of the northwest ridge of the Eggishorn and down to the **Märjelen lake**, 2300m.

Continuing to the Eggishorn: from the Märjelen lake you walk eastwards through the bottom of the Märjelenalp valley with its picturesque lakes. The Märjelen hut is here too (tunnel path into the Tälli and to the Kühboden station as a shortcut, torch needed). After the reservoir the path turns off to the right and leads to the Tälli ridge, round some bends at the end, at the point where the view opens out into the upper Rhône valley. After a short crossing over onto the east flank you meet the path coming up from Kühboden.

The following 250m are fairly steep but you are almost at the top and you can get your strength back at the Eggishorn mountain station. The short walk up the ridge on a good path to the **Eggishorn** is not strenuous, so be sure not to leave it out!

Return: by cable car to Kühboden (a good 1½ hrs on foot). If your base is on Bettmeralp, then walk back in just under one hour. Otherwise take the cable car down to Fiesch and return to your starting point with the Furka-Oberalp (FO) railway.

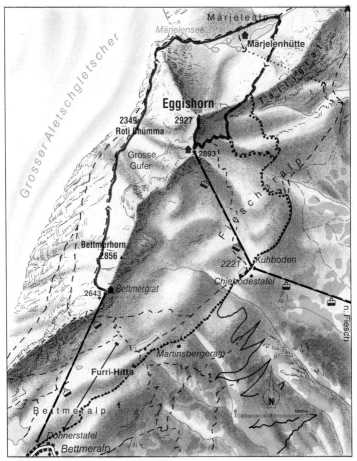

12 Aletsch forest

Views down into the Aletsch forest from a fairytale Swiss pine forest

Riederalp – Riederfurka – Aletsch forest – Blausee (blue lake) – Hoflüe – Riederalp

Location: Mörel, 759m, situated 4km above Brig at the Rotten (Rhône). FO station, regular trains, 12 minute journey from Brig.

Starting point: Riederalp, 1925m. Just like the neighbouring Bettmeralp, the old settlements in the meadows have become comfortable resorts for sport and convalescence. No cars allowed, good access from Mörel (pay car parks) with 2 cable railways (frequent service from about 5.30 to 23.00).

Walking times: Riederalp – Riederfurka ½ hr, Riederfurka – Aletsch forest – Blausee 1 hr, return via Hoflüe to Riederalp 1¼ hr.

Ascent: 370m.

Highest point: Hoflüe, 2227m.

Grade: easy walk on wide, marked paths.

Stops and accommodation: hotel and restaurant on the Riederfurka, tel. 027/9272244.

Worth seeing: Villa Cassel on the Riederfurka – first centre in Switzerland for the protection of the environment with natural history exhibition and alpine garden. The Aletsch glacier is the biggest in the Alps. The central moraines are easily visible and originate from the joining of the 3 accumulation areas of the glacier at Konkordiaplatz.

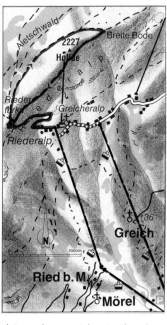

The Aletsch forest has been under complete environmental protection since 1933, i.e. no tree is to be felled, no animal hunted and no flower picked. This steeply sloping forest had almost vanished by the turn of the century due to pressures from the need for building timber and forest meadows. Since the area has been under protection there has been the recreation of a natural biotope and its continued development.

It is strictly forbidden to go off the marked paths, to pick flowers, berries and mushrooms, and of course to light fires and to smoke (a great deal of damage to the protected area was caused years ago by a forest fire)!

The protected area on the north side of the mountain ridge is clearly marked with boards. In spite of the fact that this walk is short and quite effortless,

Knotty swiss pines line the path high above the Aletsch glacier.

you can easily spend a whole day up here. Apart from the route described, there are of course other rewarding walks, all of which are very well sign-posted.

From **Riederalp** you go westwards along the broad paths to the easily visible **Riederfurka** with the hotel-restaurant and Villa Cassel 200m away. Descend only a few metres on the Aletsch side of the Furka to the **Aletsch forest** and then on the upper old moraine, almost along the forest boundary, following the good path which provides you with loads of examples of the famous, almost unsurpassable »postcard images« and magnificent Swiss pines, par-ticularly near the viewpoint just before the turn-off to Breite Bode. After this short climb there's a great view at the **Blausee** across the Rhône valley to the Valais alps.

Return: with beautiful views south-westwards, follow the ridge almost on the level via **Hoflüe** (chair lift station) and then gradually descend to the Riederfurka. Return along the ascent path to **Riederalp**.

13 Sparrhorn, 3021m

3-thousander with a princely view

Belalp – Aletschbord – Sparrhorn – Belalp

Location: Blatten, 1327m. Post bus connection with Brig (about 11 buses a day, 25 minute journey, 11km).

Starting point: Belalp, 2094m. Wide alpine pastures above the steep terrace of Blatten. Mountain station of the cable-car from Blatten (frequent service from about 7.00 to 22.00).

Walking times: Belalp mountain station – Aletschbord ½ hr, climb up to the Sparrhorn 2½ hrs, descent 2¼ hrs.

Ascent: 930m.

Grade: good marked paths through the alpine meadows, the last 250m of the path goes over precipitous and scree-covered terrain.

Stops and accommodation: several inns on the Belalp.

Worth seeing: Blatten with its old village centre and the Theoduls chapel from the 15th century. Belalp: marvellous alpine pasture covered in flowers. Impressive views down onto the Aletsch glacier and especially from the summit long distance views of Oberaletsch with the Aletschhorn.

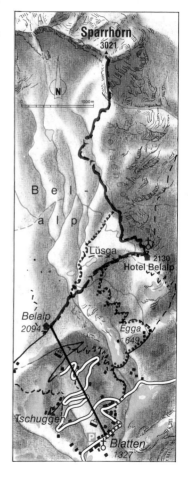

From the **Belalp** mountain station go north-eastwards, gradually ascending the track towards the Aletsch glacier. At the Belalp hotel (where you have your first striking view of the glacier tongue) you branch off left and climb up over the mountain pastures of the **Aletschbord** northwards to the beginning of the short summit section. The path winds round a few bends (with fantastic views down onto the Aletsch glacier) and finally on the loose flank just east of the

From the summit of the Sparrhorn you can see the Aletsch glacier (not visible in the picture) and the ribbon Oberaletsch glacier.
The massive three-sided Aletschhorn towers up above it. You can just make out the Oberaletsch hut on the terrace above the bend in the glacier.

ridge, to the **Sparrhorn** which, breathtakingly, drops down precipitously on its north side to the Oberaletsch glacier.

The descent is back down the same way. If you do not want to return from **Belalp** by cable-car into the valley, you can turn off at the houses of Lusgen (Lüsga, signpost, between the hotel and the Belalp station), along a narrow, very beautiful but steep path, descend to the pretty settlement of Egga and return to Blatten on a track (800m, about 1½ hrs).

14 Nesselalp – Belalp

High above Brig with views of the Aletsch glacier and the Valais Alps

Birgisch – Chittumatte – Nesselalp – Belalp – Blatten

Location and starting point: Naters, 673m. Birgisch, 1093m, on the road from Naters to Mund. Almost hourly post bus service from Brig and Mund.
Destination: Belalp, 2094m. Broad mountain pastures above the steep terrace of Blatten, cable-car station (frequent service between about 7.00 and 22.00).
Walking times: Birgisch – Chittumatte 1½ hrs, ascent to Nesselalp 1¼ hrs, ridge path to Belalp 1 hr.
Ascent: 1000m.
Highest point: Belalp, 2094m.
Grade: easy walk on good marked paths.
Stops and accommodation: inns on Belalp, no facilities on the way.
Worth seeing: on the first section of the walk, fantastic views into the bottom of Brig valley, and then from Nesselalp views of the Aletsch glacier and into the Blatten valley basin. Pretty chapel on Nesselalp.

View from Belalp over the Rhône valley to the Mischabel mountains.

From **Birgisch** climb up, gradually at first, along the old forest track towards Mund. After 500m branch off steeply right to Oberbirgisch and continue in the same direction into Birgisch forest. A rough forest track joins from the right. Continue on this upwards through the forest, cross over a track and finally reach **Chittumatte** alpine meadow clearing.

The well-laid path winds steeply up the rocky section above the alpine meadow and gives you beautiful views across the Rhône valley over to the Leone range in the Valais Alps. It soon becomes less steep and you reach the delightful mountain pastures of **Nesselalp**. It's worth going a few metres more above the huts to the precipice over the Blatten valley.

The rest of the walk is across the broad alpine slopes of Belalp to Bäll and **Belalp** station is merely a stroll now, but with magnificent views all around. From Bäll you can descend directly to Blatten, otherwise from Belalp station by cable-car into the valley. **Return** to Naters/Brig by post bus.

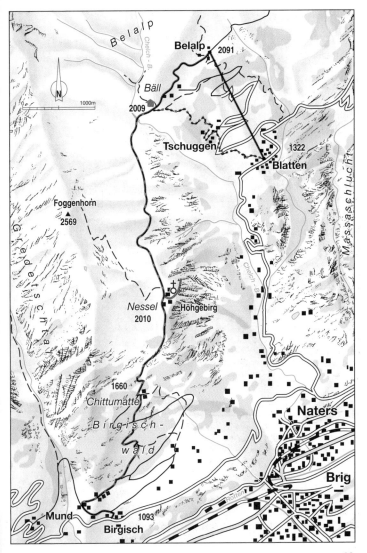

15 Stockalper path

Historic path over the Simplon pass

Brig – Simplon pass – Simplon – Furggu – Zwischbergen valley – Gondo

Location: Brig, 684m, capital of the Upper Valais, excursion centre in the Rhône valley between the Simplon and the Lötschberg lines. Easily accessible by rail (eg. Inter-City connections Genf – Mailand). Post bus connection over the Simplon pass so that you can break the walk in many places, and also easily reach the starting points and destinations of each stage of the walk.

Destination: Gondo, 855m, border town on the Simplon pass road at the end of the famous Gondo gorge. Post bus stop.

Walking times: 2 to 3 days are anticipated for this walk. For the first stage Brig – Simplon pass you should reckon on 5 to 6 hrs walking (13km, 1500m in ascent, with 200m in descent in between).

The second stage Simplon pass – Simplon village is about 9km long and 760m in descent taking about 1½ hrs.

For the third stage via Furggu into the Zwischberg valley and to Gondo you need 4 to 5 hrs (13km, 630m in ascent and 1250m in descent). If you have the stamina you can combine the second and third stages, but on the second day you should certainly take time to explore the area of the Simplon pass!

Highest point: Simplon pass, 2006m.

Grade: good, marked paths, and many cart tracks which have been restored at great cost along historic routes.

Because of its location the climate on the Simplon pass is harsher than in other places at high altitude – take note of this when choosing the right clothing.

Stops and accommodation: hotels and hospice on the Simplon pass. You can stop at the Engiloch restaurant and stay overnight in Simplon village, hotel-restaurant in Gstein-Gabi and in Zwischbergen. All open in the walking season.

Worth seeing: the Simplon pass is littered with archaeological evidence from the Bronze and Iron Ages and also from Roman times. A path over the pass has been positively dated as from 1235. Busy transportation of goods on the backs of animals began from then on.

In the 17th century Kaspar Jodok Stockalper equipped the route with supply stations and stabilised difficult sections of the route. Between 1800 and 1805 Napoleon modernised and extended the road and the line was so well-chosen that today's national highway goes over this technically brilliant achievement in many places, so that extensive sections of this former road have disappeared.

The Stockalper path, on the other hand, has been reconstructed and in the last few years has been uncovered and restored at great expense.

But not only the path itself but also buildings in the area surrounding it provide a magnificent open-air museum, unique of its kind, a perfect link between natural experience and historic information. Small exhibits, at intervals along the path, give information about an earlier way of life concerning, for example, agriculture, mining and the transport of goods.

This exhibition as a whole is called an »eco-museum« (an idea from the Sixties in France) which is the attempt at an holistic portrayal of a region's network of geographical, social and cultural aspects.

Simplon village at the foot of the Fletschhorn (right) and Weißmies (left).

Starting point is the Stockalper palace in **Brig**. Ascend the »Alte Simplonstraße«, and as you leave the village go left for a short way into »Bachstraße«, then right into »Römerstraße«. Go across meadows and then under the national highway and via Lingwurm to Brei. Ascending a little road to the south on a path winding through the steep forest above (the bends of the old path had disappeared and had to be newly marked out). The following section up the rocky slopes high above the Saltina gorge has been reconstructed at great cost and so you reach Schallberg the same way as in Stockalper's time. On your descent you can either use the restored medieval path directly to Grund or Stockalper's somewhat more comfortable alternative which crosses the Ganter stream round a long left loop and rejoins the first path in the valley of the Taferna stream. You reach the former Taferna inn and zigzag along the reconstructed road with five new bridges at the original places to the **Simplon pass**.

For 500m from here the Stockalper path lies below the modern road, so your route goes a little west from this through landscape shaped by smooth round boulders and infertile meadows to the old road which you follow to the Niwe meadows and to the »Alte Spittel«. Go for a short way along the asphalt road, then on the newly constructed hikers' path to the hamlet of Nideralp and to the Simplon road where the valley narrows at the Engiloch restaurant. Below the main road you then go along the newly exposed path with much evidence of the historic past down to Mäschihüs, then over the beautiful Napoleon stone bridge and continue to Egga. The following section as far as the **Simplon** village has been restored and paving stones and dry stone walls have been uncovered.

From Simplon village the path goes for a short way along the southern approach road then leads left down over the meadows to Gstein-Gabi. It's another few metres to the bridge over the Laggin stream. The Napoleon route through the Gondo gorge separates here (to the left) from your path into the Zwischbergen valley. You go past the old »Gsteihüs« and zigzag up the Feerberg hillside covered alternately with meadows and sections of forest, passing a pretty chapel

At **Furggu** the strenuous climb is over and you start the descent into the **Zwischbergen valley**. The track is on the slope to the right but your path follows at first the little stream, then stays on the sunny side of the valley below the Seehorn and goes, after many zigzags, past Chatzhalte to the settlement of Zwischbergen. Continue across the stream, the »Große Wasser«, and walk on the other side above the old path through the valley. Just before the steep section at Gondo, where the ruins of the former gold mine are situated, the path goes over the bridge again and directly down to **Gondo** taking a shortcut across the bends of the narrow track.

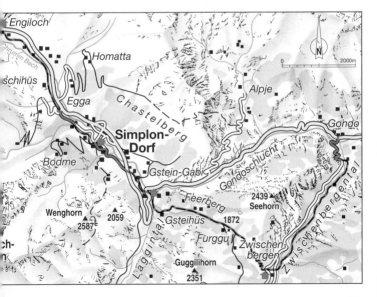

16 Folluhorn, 2656m

2000 metres above the Rhône valley – better than being in an aeroplane

Rosswald – Folluhorn – Rosswald

Location: Ried near Brig, 918m, small community on a meadow terrace on the old Simplon road above Brig. Post bus connection with Brig (about every hour between 7.00 and 19.00, journey time about 15 minutes).

Starting point: Rosswald (Glimmuschir), 1819m. An up-and-coming holiday resort high on the sunny alpine meadow terrace above the Simplon road. Marvellous views of the Bernese Alps and the mountains of the Simplon region. A narrow, twisting track leads to the village, but the houses can only be reached on foot. Cable-car to Ried (open in summer from about 7.30 to 20.00).

Parking at the station and at the pay car park in Rosswald.

Walking times: ascent from Rosswald to the Folluhorn 2¾ hrs, descent 1½ hrs.

Ascent: 840m.

Grade: easy mountain walk on well-laid paths.

Stops and accommodation: only the Saflischmatte inn on the descent , ½ hour from Rosswald.

Worth seeing: view to the Simplon pass, dominated by the enormous Fieschhorn. Wonderful views already from Rosswald into the Rhône valley down to Brig which improve as you climb up to the summit.

The path in the lower area goes through a very beautiful larch wood. The walk is remarkable for its distant views and should only be undertaken in good weather and is not recommended in poor visibility.

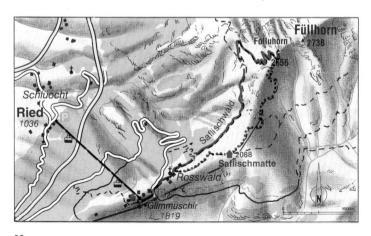

View from the ascent of Folluhorn down onto Brig.

From the mountain station in the lower area of Glimmuschir it takes a few minutes up to the car park at the end of the road. A sign points across the meadows to the upper area of **Rosswald** where you ignore the turn-off into the lift area behind the chapel on the right and go past the last houses to reach the marvellous Saflisch forest. The well-laid path can be seen from here up to the summit and leads steadily up over the forest flank and soon into the open ground of the large basin valley to the west of the Folluhorn.

Cross this flank upwards over little gullies to its northern end where you have an amazing view into the upper Rhône valley as well. Continue climbing and right at the end you zigzag a little steeper over the meadows of wild flowers, to the summit. Insatiable and sure-footed walkers can climb in 15 minutes to the somewhat higher Füllhorn, 2738m, but the magnificent view from the **Folluhorn** should enthuse even discriminating walkers sufficiently for them to spend their time enjoying the panorama from here instead!

Descent: an alternative route southwards, with beautiful views, to the Saflischmatte inn (at first intermittent tracks, then a good path) has lost much of its attraction due to the up-and-coming ski development here, but it's a vivid example of the effects of such intrusions. The usual descent route then is back down the same way.

17 Monte Leone hut, 2848m

Varied day's walk high above the Simplon pass

Simplon pass – Monte Leone hut – Mäderlücke – Rothwald

Location: Brig, 684m. Capital of the eastern Valais between Simplon and Lötschberg lines, excellent connection to the international railway network.

Starting point: Simplon pass (Kulm), 2006m. Post bus connection with Brig (about 7 a day, 30km and about 45 minute journey from Brig, 10km and 18 minute journey from Simplon village.

Destination: Rothwald, 1811m, small settlement just above the Simplon road, bus stop.

Walking times: Simplon pass – Monte Leone hut 3 hrs, hut – Mäderlücke 15 minutes, descent to Rothwald 2 hrs.

Ascent: 880m.

Highest point: Mäderlücke, 2887m.

Grade: walk on good mountain paths, marked.

Stops and accommodation: simple food in the Monte-Leone hut in the summer, tel: 027/9791412.

Worth seeing: impressive basin-shaped valley below the Chaltwasser glacier, surrounded by high peaks, ice, masses of debris and glacier chippings. There's hardly any greenery around the hut, but the colours and forms of rock strata and fields of debris make a dramatic impression beside the glacial lake. The view of the north face of Monte Leone is particularly beautiful.

From the top of the pass **Simplon**-Kulm there's a path near lift pylons across the meadows to the broader path along a water channel. Take this path through the valley and only gently uphill, past the little reservoir, and into the enormous scree basin of the Chaltwasser glacier. At about 2500m the path

View from Monte Leone down onto the Chaltwasser pass with the Wasenhorn and across the Rhône valley, the Bernese Alps with the conspicuous Bietschhorn.

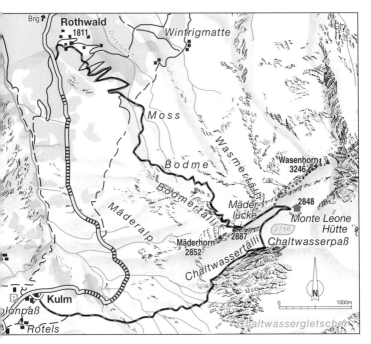

turns off left and goes over the smoothly polished slabs of the glacier outlet. It continues upwards over the moraines and then into the moraine valley (Chaltwassertälli), until you come abruptly to the edge of the plateau area of the pass. In a few minutes the path crosses above the lake to the nearby **Monte Leone hut**.

For the descent you take the path to **Mäderlücke** which traverses a little above the ascent path. It zigzags down steeply into Bodmertälli and then to the meadows of Bodmeralp. A little later there's a road along by the ski lift – not built with much sensitivity to the surroundings. After a few bends in the »Jochwald« area you can descend on a footpath directly to **Rothwald** and to the bus stop.

A detour to the **Wasenhorn** is highly recommended to every mountain walker. From the path to the Mäderlücke two tracks turn off right along a geological stratum to the ridge. The climb follows tracks on the ridge itself, at times rather feint, or through the boulders a little to the right (south) below (sections I). The view is spectacular!

18 Rossbodealp near Simplon

Near to the north face of the Fletschhorn

Egga – Rossbodealp– Rossbode – Simplon village – Egga

Location and starting point: Egga, 1588m, small hamlet on the Simplon south ramp a little above Simplon village. The building style of the stone-covered houses gives the region a real southern feeling. Post bus station of the Simplon line Brig – Domodossola. Parking at the entrance to Egga.

Walking times: Egga – Rossbodealp 1¼ hrs, walk around the alpine meadow to the glacier 1 hr, descent to Simplon village 1 hr, return to Egga 30 minutes.

Ascent: 660m.

Highest point: about 2250m on the Rossbode (Grisserna).

Grade: easy alpine meadow walk.

Stops and accommodation: in Simplon village.

Worth seeing: fascinating view of the north face of the Fletschhorn with the wildly broken Rossbode glacier.

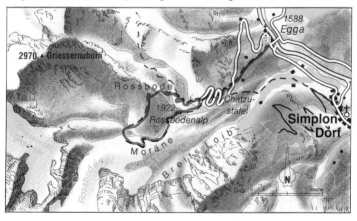

The interesting, evenly curved side moraine of the Rossbode glacier is easily reached from Rossbode. It is overgrown on this side and breaks off to the glacier almost like a petrified cornice. From here there's a good view of the different facets of a glacier in one confined space, from the ice wall of the summit region across chaotic seracs down to the debris-covered tongue. At the signpost you follow the path from **Egga** to go gradually uphill towards the forest-covered ridge. The area through which the outlets from the glacier flow on the left is called »Gletschersturz« (glacier fall), today a densely wooded field of rubble from the advance of former glaciers. At Chatzustafel, 1786m, you come close to the glacier stream and from there climb up to **Rossbodealp**, taking a shortcut from the road in the last part through a thin larch

Wild seracs of the Rossboden glacier drop down dramatically from the summit area of the Fletschhorn to the meadows.

wood. A little walk around the mountain pasture: **Rossbode** is divided by a area of broken rock which reaches up to the little moraine valley. You can see it from Rossbodealp as an almost horizontal band of meadows used for herding cattle, and there's a track leading to the upper ground with even more beautiful views. You reach this little path (cattle tracks) by climbing diagonally across the pasture.

Descent: go to the side moraine of the glacier (fine views from the moraine ridge) and continue on the good path in the moraine valley back to the alpine meadow. At Chatzustafel, turn off right along a small path across the terrain running with streams from the glacier. Go right, out onto the ridge, and across the meadows to **Simplon village**. Return to **Egga** on the valley path.

19 Seehorn, 2439m

Central vantage point over the Gondo gorge

Zwischbergen – Furggu – Seehorn – Zwischbergen

Location and starting point: Zwischbergen, 1359m, small settlement in the valley of the same name. You can drive by road from Zwischbergen as far as Furggu.

Walking times: Zwischbergen – Furggu 2 hrs, summit climb 1¾ hrs, return to Zwischbergen 2½ hrs.

Ascent: 1080m.

Grade: easy mountain walk on good path to Furggu. There's a very easy, well-trodden path to the summit.

Stops and accommodation: in Zwischbergen.

Worth seeing: Gondo gorge on the Simplon pass road, the still quiet Zwischbergen high mountain valley. High moor landscape with wonderful larch trees and a small lake near Furggu.

This walk provides almost unique views into the Weißmies range. There are also views down from the summit into the Gondo gorge and over to the south flank of Monte Leone.

From the reservoir in the valley bottom you can drive up a few more metres to the houses of **Zwischbergen** (Bord), however, because of the limited parking spaces, you should leave the car on the valley road at the signpost, a good 300m after the reservoir, and start the walk from there. In a few minutes you reach the road which takes you across the rift valley coming down from Furggu and zigzag up on its eastern side, at times through quite dense larch trees, thinning in places, to Chatzhalte, 1637m. The path continues upwards until it joins with a meadow road near **Furggu**.

The Seehorn from the Zwischbergen valley.

From Furggu to the Seehorn: at the signpost you turn off right and through the beautiful Seehalte forest with solitary ancient larch trees you reach a small moorland lake (Seetole). The path now climbs over the south west flank of the **Seehorn** where it winds round – rather strenuous middle section – to the summit with the transmitter mast which can be seen from far away.
Descent: on the same path back to Furggu. As an alternative a lovely path goes down from here north-westwards over the Feerberg to Gabi on the Simplon pass road and from there you take the post bus through the Gondo gorge to Gondo.

20 Mälch ridge, 2450m

Round walk with views high above Visp and the Baltschieder valley

Chastler – Mälch ridge – Honalpa – Chastler

Location: Brig, 684m, or Visp, 651m, the two central places in the Upper Valais. Excellent connections with the international railway network.

The Bletschhorn dominates the back of the valley.

Starting point: Chastler, 1606m, not accessible by post bus (the line from Brig ends in Mund, from there about 1½ hrs on foot, or by taxi or your own car).

A good alternative is to go from Visp by post bus to Eggerberg-Finnen (in summer about 4 a day, 35 minute journey) and ascend a lovely path in a good 30 minutes to Chastler.

Walking times: Chastler – edge of the forest 1½ hrs, ascent to the Mälch ridge 1½ hrs, descent to Honalpa 1 hr, return to Chastler 40 minutes.

Ascent: 840m.

Grade: mountain walk partly on very feint paths without waymarkers, also steep traverses on tracks. Only safe and experienced mountain walkers with a good head for heights should undertake this isolated walk.

Stops and accommodation: only at the start and the end of the walk in Chastler.

Worth seeing: fantastic views down to Visp and especially into the Baltschieder valley. Distant views into the eastern Valais – the whole chain of the Valais Alps with the Weißhorn, Mischabel and Weißmies. The windswept Swiss pines and larches at the edge of the wood are striking.

From the houses of **Chastler** follow the road or the shortcut footpath (signpost towards Brischeru), until you reach the road above the second bend. You then stay on the cart track which leads into the valley bottom and then up on the other side in the forest. About 200m from the end a small path turns off right and leads to the pretty edge of the wood. Continue uphill on the ridge with magnificent views.

The path loses itself occasionally but you can see the way ahead and you will meet some tracks again under the Mälch ridge at the latest. You could take a shortcut from the upper section on a good path under the ridge to the left onto a ledge above the rocks, but the views are worthwhile on the detour

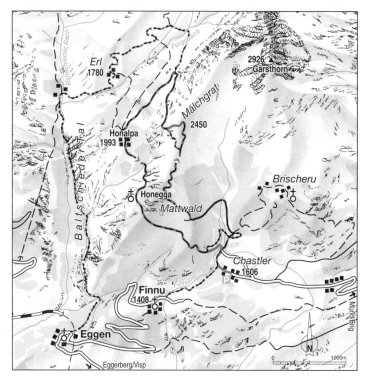

over the **Mälch ridge**. You descend on tracks from here westwards to the aforementioned ledge and meet a path which crosses the steep slope above the Baltschieder valley into the barren alpine meadow basin of the Furgg stream high above the group of houses at Erl.

About half way to the back of the valley a path turns off left down to the **Honalpa** which is visible from above. From here follow the path which leads out of the valley through the gullies of the »Pschissnugraben« to the Honegga chapel and soon meets a rough forest track on which you return to **Chastler**.

If you do not have to return to the starting point there's a particularly delightful alternative. Do not go over Honalpa back to Chastler, go instead to the Furgg stream and up steeply to Erl and down into the Baltschieder valley. Then return along the Bisse Gorperi (Walk 21) to Eggen.

21 Baltschieder valley

Effortless walking alongside masterpieces of old hydraulic engineering

Eggen – Baltschieder valley – Außerberg

Location: Visp, 651m, SBB and BVZ stations. Brig, 684m, junction with very good international rail connections.

Starting point: Eggen, 1060m. Post bus from Visp (about 10 a day, 20 minute journey, 9km). Außerberg village, 1008m. BLS station (100m below the village), post bus from Visp (about 12 a day, 20 minute journey, 10km). On the BLS stretch about 12 regional trains a day, which stop at every station, 15 minute journey from Brig to Außerberg, 18km. Parking at the railway stations of Brig and Visp as well as in Eggen.

Walking times: Eggen – Baltschieder valley (Ze Steinu) 1¼ hrs, along the Niwärch (water channel) to Salmufee 1 hr, descent to Außerberg ½ hr, 3 hrs in total.

Ascent: 230m.

Highest point: bottom of Baltschieder valley (Ze Steinu), 1287m.

Grade: not very tiring walk on good paths, if at times very exposed. Good head for heights needed, possibly a rope necessary for children! No facilities.

Worth seeing: splendid channels on the steepest rock faces, interesting views down to Visp.

The water channel from the Baltschieder valley goes across steep rock faces as well.

The paths lead along daringly laid water channels (Suonen or Bisses, in the eastern Alps also called Waale) into a wild side valley of the Rhône. Some sections run along almost vertical rock faces with the help of »Käneln« (hollowed out tree trunks). Short tunnels have been drilled in other places. Not until 1975 was Außerberg supplied with water through a 1.5km long tunnel. The old waterway »Niwärch« has since been maintained with the voluntary work of SAC members.

In **Eggen** you take the path between the uppermost houses at the signpost »Bisse Gorperi«. It goes slightly uphill into the bottom of the Teiffe stream and leads up a short way to the open water channel. Now you follow a good path, always along the outer edge of the channel and through several short tunnels into the valley – impressively, on the last kilometre, across a big rock face. On the bridge (1216m) you cross over the Baltschieder valley and climb on the other side about 60m up to the water channel. It's certainly worth walking a little bit further into **Baltschieder valley** to Ze Steinu and if there's enough time, to the chapel of Eültini (a good ½ hr). Back at the water channel leave the turn-off onto the tunnel path to the left below you and follow the Niwärch. At first, still on the steep overgrown valley side, the path leads daringly across rock faces and deep gullies. Then you reach the end of the channel at Salmufee (1259m, the tunnel also leads to a point nearby) and walk down to **Außerberg** on the track.

22 Bietsch valley

Nature and technology – here in perfect harmony

St. German – Riedgarto – Bietsch valley – Ritzubode – railway viaduct – St. German

Location and starting point: St. German, 757m, idyllic village above the vineyards in the Rhône valley. Post bus from Visp (about 10 a day, 15 minute journey, 8km). Parking in Visp and at the start of St. German village (few spaces).

Walking times: St. German – Riedgarto 45 minutes, Riedgarto – Bietsch valley 30 minutes, Bietsch valley – Ritzubode – BLS viaduct 15 minutes, viaduct – St. German 1 hr. Total time 3 hrs.

Ascent: 350m.

Highest point: Ritzubode, 1090m.

Grade: effortless walk on very good paths.

Stops and accommodation: kiosk at the tunnel entrance below the huts of Ritzubode, open around June to October in the walking season.

Worth seeing: impressive walk into the ravine-like Biestch valley. The intriguing railway viaduct between the portals of the tunnel on either side of the steep valley, which you cross over on foot at a height of

over 70m on the return path, will even impress non-railway enthusiasts, particularly if a train thunders past at the same time! You will find more historic water channels across breathtaking steep walls even in this valley.

The whole of the path on the Lötschberg south ramp from Hohtenn to Außerberg, Eggerberg or eventually to Lalden is highly recommended, but is however a full day's trip (information from all BLS railway counters). The path was constructed by the BLS for the building of the railway line by using the old water channels and paths and is marked throughout. It certainly is not to be recommended for those who love solitude – it is full of walkers even in the high season. The section of the walk described here is one of the most interesting and because it is short, can be enjoyed at any time of the day.

The walk begins at the western end of **St. German**. It leads quickly round two steep bends up to the water channel and then immediately afterwards to **Riedgarto**, a beautiful area of rock fall with marvellous resting and viewing places. The biggest part of the climb is already behind you. Now you go into the valley along the fairly level, broad path to the viaduct. Leave this to your

The Bietsch valley bridge looks as if it's part of a model railway.

left and continue to the natural bridge over the deep ravine of the Bietsch stream. Climb a short way up on the other side to the path leading into the back of the **Bietsch valley**. Heading out of the valley again, a good 100m above the viaduct, to **Ritzubode** at the exit of the Bietsch valley, a short descent to the railway tunnel brings you to the kiosk. Just below the next lower bend of the road to Raron the path turns off at a signpost into the Bietsch valley again and leads through several tunnels back to the **viaduct**.

You can cross the gorge directly by the side of the rails and then take the ascent path again to return to **St. German**.

23 Heida vineyard path

Nature trail to the highest vineyard in middle Europe

Visp – Bächji – Hotee – Visperterminen

Location and starting point: Visp, 651m, small town at the entry of the Vispa into the Rhône valley, junction of the railway to Zermatt and the roads to Täsch and Saas Fee.

Destination: Visperterminen, about 1340m. Post bus connection with Visp (frequent time-table, about 9 buses a day, 25 minute journey, 10km).

Walking times: Visp – Bächji ½ hr, Bächji – Hotee (path through vineyards) 1¼ hrs, Hotee – Visperterminen 1 hr. Total time 2½ – 3 hrs.

Ascent: 690m.

Highest point: Visperterminen, 1340m.

Grade: easy walk on good, marked paths.

Stops and accommodation: inns in Visp, Staldbach and Visperterminen.

Worth seeing: there are information boards in the vineyard about the types of wine. The most important of the white wines are the Chasselas, Gutedel (Fendant), Gros Rhin (Johannisberg) and the Heida, the oldest grape variety in the Valais. Amongst the reds, the Pinot Noir, which combined with the Gamay, gives the famous and popular Dôle.

Ober- and Unterstalden are small hamlets still preserving their old style and Visperterminen also offers a scenic, old village centre with narrow alleyways between the houses. In Unterstalden can be found the St. Jodern winery which as a self-help organisation for Visperterminen helps safeguard the survival of small winegrowers, since the wine industry suffers greatly from over-production even in Switzerland. Those interested can enquire about guided tours and wine tastings at Visp tourist office. If you prefer to be out on the hills you can travel by bus to Visperterminen where a sign at the bus stop marks the start of the Heida vineyard path.

You leave the old village centre of **Visp** southwards, past the cemetery, to the first vineyard (Hubel, sign). A little below the road to Visperterminen the path

Each square metre of cultivated land has to be carved out of the mountain.

goes through the vines into the **Bächji** valley and crosses over the road in the bottom (from here there's a 10 minute detour to the winery). Now you go round big bends on a broad path through the highest vineyard in Europe. You will find interesting information about wine growing in this region on boards.

You reach the forest at the top and the **Hotee** clearing (Hohtenn) with wonderful views. The path ascends for a short while, then leads almost on the level to **Visperterminen**.

24 Gebidum pass, 2201m

Effortless walk to an interesting view point

Giw – Gebidum pass – Visperterminen

Location: Visperterminen, about 1340m, beautiful settlement in a panoramic location high above the Visp valley. Post bus connection with Visp (frequent buses, about 9 a day, 30 minute journey, 13km).

Starting point: Giw mountain station, 1976m, for the cable-car from Visperterminen. Restaurant.

Walking times: Giw – Gebidum pass ¾ hr, descent to Visperterminen 1¾ hrs.

Ascent: 225m in ascent, 860m in descent.

Grade: good paths, but a short section above Giw has unfortunately been damaged when they built a ski slope.

Worth seeing: interesting views over the Matter valley to the Weißhorn mountains opposite, and also from the pass into the remote Nanz valley.

Water channel from the Nanz valley to the pass. Wonderful forest path to the Antonius chapel. The old centre of Vieperterminen is worth visiting.

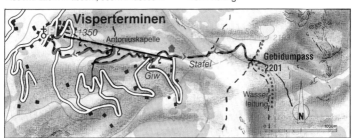

This walk goes onto the panoramic high ridge of the Gebidum which pushes forward from the Weißhorn range as far as the Rhône valley. The descent past the Antonius chapel leads through a particularly beautiful mountain forest (Kapellenweg).

From the **Giw** mountain station the broad path goes for a short way above the ugly ski slope eastwards to Stafel and then across open ground to the **Gebidum pass**. It's certainly worth going another few metres into the Nanz valley along an old water channel and you should not miss out a detour to the marvellous lake on the pass! It's a short return to the station and then you follow the wonderful footpath round a few bends through the Bann forest above **Visperterminen** to the Antonius chapel. At the edge of the forest, along by the meadows under the ski-lift, you descend to the tarmac road and return along this to Visperterminen.

View across Moosalp to Visperterminen with Monte Leone above.

25 Gsponer ridge path

Viewing balcony high above the Saas valley

Gspon – Finilu alpine meadow – Lindeboden – Kreuzboden – Saas Grund

Location: Stalden, about 800m, situated above the merging of the Vispa valleys,

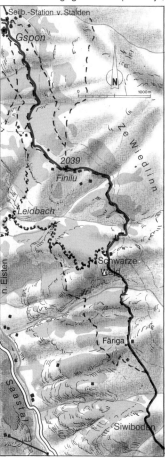

old village centre. Saas Grund, 1559m, main village in the Saas valley. Bus connection with Visp via Stalden.

Starting point: Gspon, 1893m, small settlement high above Stalden. Not accessible by car, cable-car from Stalden (frequent service). A few parking places in Stalden, better in Visp and then by bus or train to and from Stalden.

Walking times: Gspon – Oberfinilu ¾ hr, to the Lindeboden 1½ hrs, final stage to the Kreuzboden station 2 hrs. Total time 4 to 5 hrs.

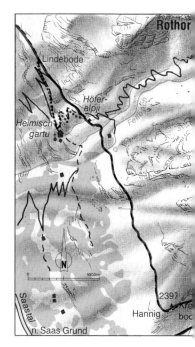

The huts of Bord with a view of the Balfrin mountains.

Ascent: 510m.
Highest point: about 2400m, just before reaching Kreuzboden.
Grade: broad paths with sufficient waymarkers. Not very tiring despite its length (12.5km).
Stops and accommodation: inns in Gspon. Restaurant at Kreuzboden station. Restaurant Heimischgarten, 2100m, reached by a 10 minute descent from Lindeboden (open in summer, overnight stop available, tel: 027/9572920), return to the ridge path in a good 20 minutes.
Worth seeing: chapel with beautiful crucifix in Gspon dating from 1694. Wonderful views deep into the Saas valley and of the Mischabel mountains. Interesting water channel system.

From the cable-car station in **Gspon** follow a broad path southwards across flowering alpine meadows to the larch and Swiss pine forest which you pass through fairly on the level to the huts of Bord. Immediately behind them, at **Finilualp**, the path goes uphill for a while and then crosses some steep gullies along the elaborately laid water channel. You come to the marvellously situated Obere Schwarze Wald hut (possible steep descent to Eisten) and pass through some more deep valleys to reach the Mattwaldalp with the Färiga alpine hut. After crossing the Mattwald stream you come to the alpine plain of Siwiboden and through a beautiful rocky area to the picturesque **Lindeboden**. Continue right down to the bottom of the Fell stream which, in the past, has severely threatened Saas Balen with floodwater. On the recently constructed section of path below the Jegihorn you eventually reach Kreuzboden station for the **Saas Grund** cable-car, with increasingly fine views into the basin-shaped valley of Saas Fee.
Return by cable-car or descend the valley on foot (about 1½ hrs).

26 Almagelleralp ridge path – Kreuzboden

Viewing balcony opposite the 4-thousanders of the Mischabel chain

Saas Almagell – Almageller Alp mountain hut – Kreuzboden – Saas Grund

Location and starting point: Saas Almagell, 1672m. Quiet holiday resort in the Saas valley. Post bus connection to Saas Grund (about every hour, 8 minute journey). Connection with the post bus line to Saas Fee and Visp.

Walking times: Saas Almagell – Almageller Alp mountain hut 1¾ hrs, ridge path to Kreuzboden 3 hrs, descent via Trift to Saas Grund 2¼ hrs.

Ascent: 840m.

Highest point: about 2480m.

Grade: undemanding mountain walk on good paths, though you have to cross a fairly steep flank at the Weißflue – the path is good here as well, but you need to be sure-footed and have a good head for heights.

Stops and accommodation: Almageller Alp mountain hut, 2194m (open in summer, restaurant, overnight facilities in rooms and group accommodation. Tel: 027/9571179). Kreuzboden station restaurant, 2397m. Trift mountain pasture, 2072m (open in summer, restaurant and overnight facilities).

Worth seeing: fantastic view of the Mischabel chain already on the climb up to Almageller Alp, the view opens out magnificently later on the ridge path.

An overnight stop on the Almagelleralp is not necessary for this walk, but is highly recommended. This means that you make a comfortable start on the ridge walk early in the morning and enjoy the especially beautiful morning light on the mountains opposite. To save your knees on the difficult and yet delightful walk down to Saas Grund, take the cable-car from Kreuzboden.

The path begins in **Saas Almagell** at the car park below the gorge of the Almagell stream and winds up through wispy larch trees to the Chüelbrunnji

The Almageller Alp mountain hut with the Portjen ridge mountains.

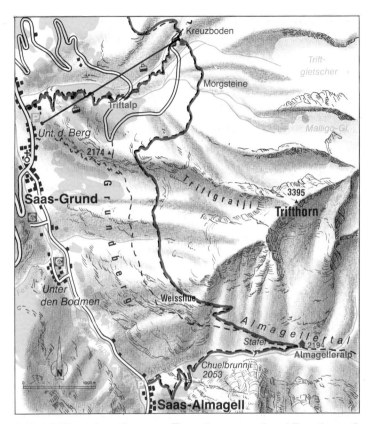

bridge, 2053m, above the gorge. The path goes gently uphill on the north side of the stream to the **Almageller Alp** mountain hut. Continue from the hut over the meadow to above the rocks of the Weißflue where the horizontal traverse along a new track to the Trift basin begins (the deeper old path should not be used any more). Eventually above Triftalp, you descend gradually to **Kreuzboden** station.

Descend on foot via Triftalp to Saas Grund: Go down on the footpath, at the beginning near the track, then over the meadow area to the Trift huts. From here you zigzag down steeply through the beautiful larch forest directly to **Saas Grund**.

27 Monte Moro pass, 2870m

To the most famous viewing point of the highest rock face in the Alps, the east face of the Monte Rosa

Mattmark reservoir – Tälliboden – Monte Moro pass – Mattmark reservoir

Location: Saas Almagell, 1672m. Quiet holiday resort in the Saas valley. Post bus connection with Saas Grund (about every hour, 8 minute journey), link with the post bus lines to Saas Fee and Visp.

Starting point: top end of the wall of the Mattmark reservoir, 2210m, in summer road and bus connection from Saas Almagell (about 10 a day, 17 minute journey, 9km). Parking in Saas Almagell and at the top end by the wall.

Walking times: reservoir wall – Tällioboden 1¾ hrs, from there to the pass 1 hr. Total time just under 3 hrs. About 1¾ to 2 hrs on the descent.

Ascent: 660m.

Grade: undemanding mountain walk (track to the southern end of the lake), marked path from Tälliboden to the pass (old trading route from the 13th century).

Stops and accommodation: Rifugio Città di Malnate, situated a good 5 minutes to the west under the top of the pass on the Italian side (do not forget your passport), mountain station of the Macugnaga cablecar.

Worth seeing: east face of the Monte Rosa massif, the highest rock and ice face in the whole of the Alps. The Monte Moro pass has been a well-used crossing point for many centuries. The upper Macugnaga valley was inhabited by people from the Valais and a few relics have survived until today, especially in the architectural style of old houses and in the names of features in the local landscape.

The east wall of the Monte Rosa is usually hidden behind clouds very early on fine summer days (cloud formation almost always starts in the

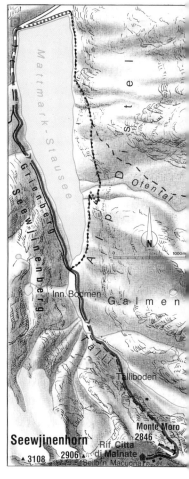

Monte Moro pass, viewing point for the Monte Rosa east face.

Monte Moro pass area). From midday onwards most of the wall is also in shade. A relatively early start in the valley is therefore advisable so that you are on top at the latest between 9 and 10!

From the top end of the wall of the **Mattmark reservoir** you go along the track on the western bank of the lake gently uphill through two short tunnels and then almost on a level to the southern end – the meadows of the slope, called Grienberg, on the western edge are well-known for the many beautiful flowers.

At the bridge take the path leading further up the valley (the 3 hours walking time given here is surely not right). A moderate incline brings you into the Tälli and after another bridge to the **Tälliboden**. More signs are marked on a large boulder and they point unmistakably to the rock-strewn flank of the Monte Moro across which the historic path from the middle ages leads on natural terraces and elaborate slab steps almost in a straight line to the **Monte Moro pass**.

A little west above the deepest cleft a large statue stands on the border ridge and marks a particularly beautiful viewing point. A little south the Rifugio Città di Malnate can bee seen.

The **descent** goes back the ascent path. However at the reservoir you are recommended to take the path along the eastern edge, adding another 150m of climbing. The rewards are even more attractive views of the Strahl-horn and you extend the walk by hardly more than 20 minutes.

28 Britannia hut, 3030m and Klein Allalin, 3070m

A geological and mineralogical walk with splendid views

Saas Fee – Plattjen – Heidefridhof – Britannia hut – Klein Allalin – Egginerjoch – Felskinn

Location and starting point: Saas Fee, 1790m. Saas Fee itself does not allow cars, but at the start of the village there are large pay car parks and multi-storey car parks. Post bus connection with Visp via Saas Grund (about every hour between 6.30 and 19.30). Plattjen mountain station, 2570m, cable-car from Saas Fee-Kalbermatten (open from beginning of July to the middle of October).

Walking times: bus stop – valley station ¼ hr, ascent to the Plattjen mountain hut 1½ hrs, to the mountain station 20 minutes, mountain station – Britannia hut 2 hrs, detour to the Klein Allalin ¼ hr, Britannia hut – Felskinn station ¾ hr. Total time 4½ hrs, if you use the Plattjen cable-car, 2¾ hrs.

Ascent: depending on your starting point, 500 to 1280m.

Grade: well marked paths. The small Chessjen glacier has no crevasses and is not steep so you can normally walk on it quite easily with good footwear. Broad track to the Felskinn station above the upper part of this glacier always present.

Stops and accommodation: Plattjen mountain hut, 2411m (private, with a warden in summer, no accommodation). Britannia hut, 3030m (SAC, food and accommodation available – booking necessary), Felskinn station, 2991m (restaurant).

Worth seeing: Saas Fee – pretty village square, glacier cave. Wonderful view from Plattjen into the valley basin of Saas Fee and the Vispa valley, rock formations on Egginer. Metro-Alpin (underground railway) from Felskinn to Mittelallalin, fabulous panoramic view, revolving restaurant, ice cave.

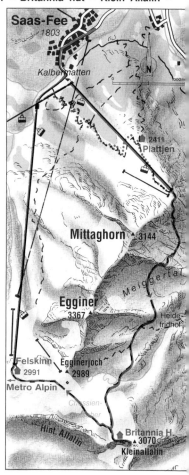

Steinbocks on Heidefridhof with the Weißmies mountains in the background.

The path under the Egginer massif was constructed as a geological trail. The interesting geology of this region stems from the collision of two surfaces, i.e. from different rock systems.

From the valley station in the **Saas Fee-Kalbermatten** area of the village you go towards the Fee glacier for a few metres, then a path branches off left at the edge of a firebreak and leads round many bends to the mountain hut. From there a broad path goes parallel to the cable-car not too steeply anymore to **Plattjen** mountain station. In a few steps you reach an enormous boulder field with a particularly beautiful view into the Saas valley. The path is well-marked through piles of debris and continues on a grassy strip under the Mittaghorn into the broad cirque of the Meigger valley. It's a comfortable walk on the other side to the **Heide Fridhof**, a marvellous place to take a rest and enjoy the views. Walk along a short strip into the scree basin under the Chessjen glacier and climb diagonally across up to the nearby **Britannia hut**.

Detour to the **Klein Allalin**: from the hut descend a short way eastwards onto the col and across the ridge, which is sometimes covered in snow and at the top covered in debris, to the summit close by.

Crossing to the **Egginerjoch** and **Felskinn station**: a broad track in the snow leads almost on the level under the rocks of the Hinterallalin over to the Joch, then swings to the west until you are above the station and finally descends a short way down to it.

29 Balfrinalp ridge path

Interesting ridge path below the Balfrin

Saas Bidermatten – Stafelalp – Sengboden – Saas Bidermatten

Location and starting point: Saas Bidermatten, 1540m. Settlement west of the Saaser Vispa between Saas Balen and Saas Grund. The hamlet consists almost exclusively of old Valais houses and winding alley ways. Good bus connections from Stalden/Visp and Saas Fee (every hour between about 6.30 and 19.30).
Parking on the road before the village, but not in the village itself.

Walking times: Saas Bidermatten – Saas Bidermatten – Stafelalp 1¾ hrs, Stafelalp – Senggboden ¾ hr, descent to Bidermatten ¾ hr.

Ascent: 660m.

Highest point: Stafelalp, bridge over the Schutz stream, 2197m.

Grade: good, sufficiently marked paths. No refreshments or accommodation.

Worth seeing: Bidermatten, a small settlement, preserved in its original style. Marvellous trees in the treeline area. Remains of an old aqueduct near the Senggboden. Beautiful views of the Weißmies range almost all of the way.

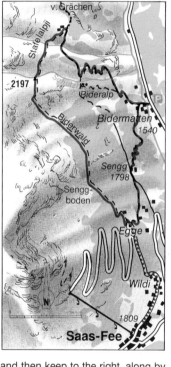

This walk goes between Stafelalp and Senggboden along part of the magnificent Grächen ridge path over the Seetal pass to Saas Fee (see Walk 30).

From the Vispa bridge you go up through the village **Saas Bidermatten** and then keep to the right, along by the edge of the forest, to the upper bridge over the Bider stream. Now the path climbs diagonally right up the slope and crosses the gully of the Schutz stream – leave the turn-offs to Bideralp on your left. The path now winds up through a light wood to the Schwarzbergweid and then, gently ascending, crosses into the nearby northern trench, where, on the far side, the **Stafelalp** huts are to be found – wonderful, picturesque larch trees and Swiss pines cover this part of the slope.

View from Balfrinalp down to Saas Grund, with the Weißmies mountains above.

Return to Bidermatten across the Senggboden: the path now ascends for a little way to the southwest until you finally reach the treeline. It leads almost on a level through the basin-shaped valley with the outlet of the Bider glacier and then descends steadily along an old aqueduct through the Bider forest to the **Senggboden**. You continue for another good kilometre, gradually descending to the Egge clearing where the path to Saas Fee (a 20 minute walk) branches off. Now descend until you can walk almost on the level again northwards to Sengg. Cross over the road and zigzag steeply down to the valley floor. The path eventually leads along the edge of the forest back to **Saas Bidermatten**.

30 Seetal pass, 2980m

Impressive walk high above the Vispa valleys

Seetalhorn mountain railway station – Seetal pass – Balfrinalp – Hannigalp

Location and starting point: Grächen, about 1600m. Bus connection with St. Niklaus (14 buses a day, 25 minute journey, 9km). Pay car parks in the village. Seetalhorn mountain railway station, 2870m.

Walking times: mountain station – Seetal pass ½ hr, descent to Balfinalp 1 hr, continuing to Hannigalp 2¼ hrs. Total time just under 4 hrs.

Ascent: about 200m. Descent 900m.

Grade: at times steep terrain, but not difficult.

Stops and accommodation: restaurants at the mountain railway stations.

Worth seeing: beautiful barn in Grächen. Old aqueducts to the meadows and fields. A small picturesque lake a little way above the village.

Comment: we recommend that experienced mountain walkers take the narrow marked path from Balfinalp which runs, above the described walk, along grassy cornice-like strips on the very steep eastern slope of the Distelhorn. There is also an interesting connecting path from Balfrinalp to Walk 29 and further on to Saas Fee.

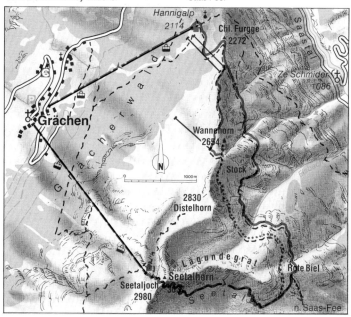

View of the Weißhorn from the Seetal pass.

The summit ridge round the Seetalhorn is in a condition of the utmost decay, the monolithic summit rocks seem to fly in the face of all laws of gravity and tower over both sides of a huge sea of rubble – the See valley on the east side reminds you of a moon landscape. The long traverse under the Distelhorn gives you especially good views into the Saas valley and of the summit of the Weißmies range.

From the **Seetalhorn mountain railway station** you zigzag along the path through the pile of rubble to the **Seetal pass**, 2980m. On the other side descend a little steeper for just a few metres, then at a more pleasant gradient on the north side of the rubble-filled See valley to the lower end of the Lägunde ridge on **Balfrinalp** (Rote Biel high alpine meadow), where the path to Saas Fee turns off, as well as the alpine alternative walk to the Wannehorn (see above). The pleasant path now leads into the basin-shaped valley of the Eistbach, at times across breathtakingly steep slopes, and on the other side round the Stock where the views are outstanding. Go across the east side of the Wannhorn to reach the ridge of Hannigalp and the forest boundary with particularly fine Swiss pines. A few more steps and you are back at the cable-car station to return to Grächen (alternatively, about 1¼ hrs on foot).

31 Grathorn, 2273m

Interesting climb to the striking viewpoint above the Matter valley

Gasenried – Schalbettu – Grathorn – Gasenried

Location and starting point: Gasenried, 1659m, small settlement at the south end of the Grächener sun terrace high above St. Niklaus. Bus connection with St. Niklaus (about 7 buses a day, 25 minute journey, 8km), small car park in the village.

Walking times: Gasenried – Grathorn 2 hrs, 1¼ hrs on the descent.

Ascent: 620m.

Grade: well-signposted walk, but some parts fairly steep. No refreshments or accommodation.

Worth seeing: Gasenried has still managed to maintain its century-old village character despite the tourist building boom. The meadows and fields wrenched from the steep slopes are evidence of the arduous mountain farming which still continues. The Grathorn has been the starting or finishing point of one of the most extreme ridge paths in the Alps since 1996. As a definite mountain climb it connects Grächen with Zermatt above the Matter valley – very

alpine! Fantastic view of the Weisshorn range, especially of the Brunegghorn as well as towards the Bernise Alps.

From **Gasenried** go along the little level street for 5 minutes to the small Schalbettu chapel. Here you follow the path sign-posted »Bordierhütte« over the outlet of the Ried glacier, another few metres almost on the level on the other side, until a little path branches off to the left at a signpost and winds up steeply through the light wood. Go up, through the outlet of an avalanche gully until you come close to the left lateral moraine of the Ried glacier. Just before you reach this point a path turns off to the right away from the approach to the Bordier hut and crosses the steep flank diagonally upwards. You cross the avalanche gully again further up and eventually come out onto the open flat area where the **Grathorn** cross stands above the western corner.

If you climb another 200m southeast onto the 2474m high rounded hilltop you have a breathtaking view down onto the Ried glacier between the Balfrin and Nadelhorn ranges.

The **descent** is normally back down the ascent path. A demanding alternative is to descend the path to the south on the west flank of the mountain to the old Grat alpine hut, 2224m. There you follow a steep and, in places, unclear

From the summit plateau of the Grathorn there are beautiful views of the Weißhorn mountains.

path with very few signs which leads below the precipices of the Grathorn to an aqueduct. Continue on this till you reach a broad path again back to Schalbettu and Gasenried.

32 Tufteren ridge path

There's no nicer way to approach Zermatt

Täsch – Täschalp – Tufteren – Sunnegga – Zermatt

Location: Täsch, 1450m, at the end of the road from Visp, large pay car parks. Bus service to Visp, frequent shuttle service to Zermatt.
Starting point: Täschalp, 2214m. Parking. Small summer settlement in the Täsch valley, inn and small chapel. Reached along a very narrow little road from Täsch (also taxi bus service).
Walking times: ascent from Täsch to Täschalp 2½ hrs, Täschalp – Tufteren 2 hrs, Tufteren – Sunnegga 30 minutes, Sunnegga – Findeln – Zermatt 1¼ hrs.

Total time a good 6 hrs, about 4 hrs without ascent to Täschalp (direct descent from the alpine pasture Tufteren, 2215m, to Zermatt, 1616m ¾ hr).
Highest point: about 2350m.
Grade: easy mountain walk on good paths.
Stops and accommodation: restaurants on Täschalp and Tufteren, summer opening. Sunnegga restaurant.
Worth seeing: the most famous and also the most beautiful mountains around Zermatt can be seen from their »best side« on this walk.

If you want to save yourself the climb up to Täschalp you can also go up by taxibus. From Sunnegga it's possible to descend to Zermatt by rail but then you will miss out on some beautiful views.

From the station go eastwards through **Täsch** towards the little gorge of the Täsch stream. The path begins directly by the uppermost bridge in the village and winds up across the steep meadow slope past the Täschberg. Cross the road just before Eggestadel, then, always keeping close to the stream, go through this valley less steeply to Täschalp.

Picturesque trees at the edge of the forest along this path to Zermatt.

Tufteren ridge path: continue on Täschalp (Ottavan) about another 200m along the valley and cross the stream at a bridge. A path over the Ober Sattla branches off here while the fairly level ridge path leads out of the valley across the north slope of the Sattelspitz. Then high above Täsch turn southwards and continue, at times through marvellous larch trees, along the forest boundary and with beautiful views of the Matterhorn, to the alpine meadows of **Tufteren**. Here you can descend directly to Zermatt on a beautiful forest path, but we would recommend you to continue along the effortless path via **Sunnegga**, at the same time getting a good view of the Findel glacier region. A good path leads from the Sunnegga mountain station past the lovely Lei lake down to Findeln and eventually via Winkelmatten to **Zermatt**.

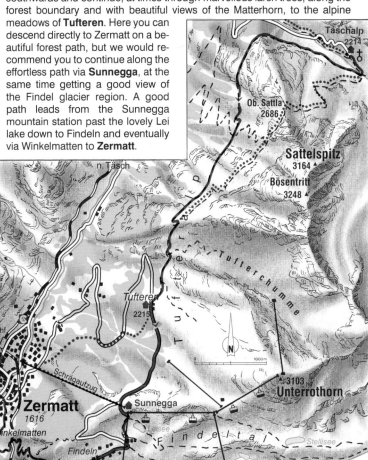

33 Oberrothorn, 3415m

High point for hikers above Zermatt

Unterrothorn – Furggji – Oberrothorn – Fluealp – Blauherd

Location: Zermatt, 1616m, world famous mountaineering resort at the foot of the Matterhorn. Access by the Zermatt rail (BVZ), also taxibus from Täsch.

Cars are not allowed in Zermatt, pay car parks in Täsch, free car parks in Visp for train passengers.

Starting point: Unterrothorn, 3103m, cable-car mountain station from Zermatt via Sunnegga and Blauherd. The valley station is situated by the Vispa directly opposite the Gornergrat railway, open in high summer between about 8.00 and 18.00, also sunrise trips with breakfast buffet in the mountain restaurant.

Walking times: Unterrothorn – Furggji 20 minutes, ascent to the summit 1½ hrs, descent to Fluealp 1½ hrs, Fluealp – Blauherd station ¾ hr.

Ascent: 430m.

Grade: easy mountain walk on good paths, free of snow in normal conditions in summer in spite of the altitude .

Stops and accommodation: Unterrothorn mountain restaurant, 3103m (open during cable-car operation times, no accommodation, tel: 027/9672675). Fluealp tourist house, 2618m (restaurant and accommodation, open in summer, tel: 027/9672551). Restaurant in Sunnegga, tel: 027/9673046.

Worth seeing: just like the Mettelhorn on the other side of the valley (Walk 36) this summit offers excellent views due to its location – the wild rocky slopes of the Dom and Täschhorn, across the firn summit between Allalinhorn, Monte Rosa and Breithorn to the Matterhorn, which reveals its perfect symmetry from here, and further towards the peaks of the Weißhorn range.

This walk not only goes onto the highest summit described in this guide, but onto one of the highest summits in the Alps accessible to walkers. The ascent is made a lot easier by the high elevation of the starting point, a fact which is endorsed by the large number of tourists. However, make sure you

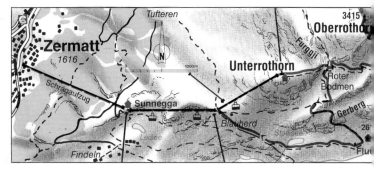

The symbol of Switzerland from its most beautiful side.

take all the necessary equipment with you, even in high summer. Even in tropical temperatures in the valley a small cloud and a light breeze are enough for the temperature immediately to drop below freezing point at this altitude.

You should never forget that up here, all year round, precipitation falls as snow and then the normally good paths very quickly become not only slippery but also harder to find.

The whole area around the Unterrothorn has been heavily reshaped for downhill skiing and regretfully serves as an illustration of the detrimental effect of mass tourism.

From the **Unterrothorn** station you descend eastwards across the broad, almost bare ridge to the **Furggji**. The path then crosses the south flank of the Oberrothorn and winds up its southeast ridge. Finally you climb over the broad and scree-covered summit ridge to the highest point of the **Oberrothorn**.

Descent over Fluealp to Blauherd station: keep to the ascent path as far as Furggji then descend southwards across infertile alpine terrain (Roter Bodmen) to the Flue along a path which leads skilfully through some broken-up rock near Gerberg.

You reach the Fluealp hut shortly afterwards where you will find pleasant accommodation and marvellous views. From Fluealp you follow the broad path to **Blauherd** station, with only the tiniest bit of uphill climbing past the picturesque Stelli lake. Return to Zermatt by cable-car or on foot via Sunnegga (Walk 32).

34 Gornergrat, 3135m

Descent to the glacier with an enormous backdrop and only a few steps away from the hustle and bustle

Gornergrat – Gorner glacier – Rotenboden

Location: Zermatt, 1616m. Rail connection from Täsch, where there's a large pay car park. Free car parking in Visp for BVZ passengers.
Starting point: Gornergrat station, 3135m (hotel, overnight stops, observatory, end station of the rack railway from Zermatt which also offers interesting and favourable price deals from Visp).
Walking times: Gornergrat – Gorner glacier 1 to 1¼ hrs, glacier – Rotenboden station 1 to 1½ hrs.
Descent: 380m. Ascent just under 200m.
Grade: easy walk on a narrow path at first

(you need to be sure-footed on the descent to the glacier). Return on broad path.
Stops and accommodation: Kulm hotel at Gornergrat (restaurant, rooms, tel: 027/9666400), restaurants in Zermatt and Täsch.
Worth seeing: Gornergrat, the most famous and the most visited viewing point of the Alps, unique panorama of the 4 thousanders around Zermatt. You can travel further by cable-car to the Stockhorn, 3405m. Deep views onto the Gorner and Grenz glaciers with an arctic feel. Guided nature and wildlife walks.

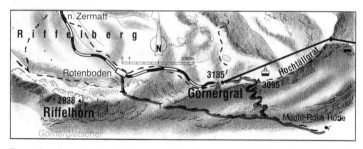

From the uppermost walled area of the **Gornergrat station** descend gently eastwards in 5 minutes to the 3095m point where the descent south begins and then winds down more deeply, at one point through an easy rocky area, to the path from Rotenboden to the Monte-Rosa hut. Go along this path eastwards to the magnificent meeting point of the **Gorner and Grenz glaciers** (turn round point). You can see the Monte-Rosa hut 2.5km southeast on the moraine, but walking across the glacier to the hut requires some alpine experience (marked path). Return to Rotenboden: the broad, well-marked path goes gently down across the slopes of the Gornergrat to **Rotenboden** station. The ibex herd long ago settled here, is only a little shy.

Gornergrat station, a worthwhile destination for visitors to Zermatt.

35 Höhbalmen ridge path

Viewing balcony for the north face of the Matterhorn

Zermatt – Trift mountain hut – Höhbalmstafel – Zmutt glacier – Zermatt

Location and starting point: Zermatt, 1616m. World famous mountaineering and winter sports' resort at the end of the Matter valley. No cars are allowed in the town, rail connection with Brig/Visp via Täsch. Pay car park in Täsch. Frequent service of the BVZ Täsch – Zermatt. Free car parking at the station for rail passengers. Taxis Täsch – Zermatt. Your starting point is the station in Zermatt.

Walking times: Zermatt – Trift mountain hut 2¼ hrs, Trift mountain hut – Höhbalmstafel 1 hr, Höhbalmstadel – Zmutt glacier 1½ hrs, continuing to Zermatt 2½ hrs.
Ascent: 1170m.

Highest point: Schwarzläger, 2788m.
Grade: walk on good, well-marked mountain paths.
Stops and accommodation: Alterhaupt (Hotel Edelweiss), 1961m. Trift mountain hut, 2337m (overnight stops, both places are open in summer). Zmutt, 1936m (inn).
Worth seeing: Trift gorge, Trift glacier basin below Obergabelhorn and Zinalrothorn. From Höhbalmstafel there are open views of Strahlhorn, Monte Rosa and Breithorn, but especially of the north faces of the Matterhorn and Dent d'Hérens! Meadows full of flowers.

The climb from **Zermatt station** to the **Trift mountain hut** through the interesting Trift gorge is described in Walk 36.

Ridge path above Höhbalmen: from the **Trift mountain hut** take the path leading to the Trift stream and climb up under the rocks of the Triftflue, zigzagging up a little at first, to the Höhbalmstadel, 2610m point.

Already most of the difficult climbing is behind you now and you can enjoy especially good views over the whole of the Zermatt valley basin from the Mischabel range as far as the Monte Rosa and Breithorn massifs.

Now the path goes over the terrace-like alpine meadows of the Höhbalmen to the southwest and then to the west high above the Zmutt glacier valley and directly opposite the Matterhorn north face. At Schwarzläger you have reached the highest point of the walk and the path now descends and winds

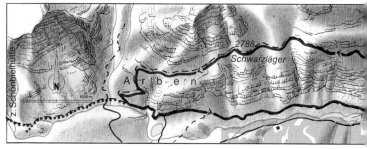

Dent d'Hérens, silent neighbour of the Matterhorn above the Zmutt glacier.

down to the lateral moraine of the broad **Zmutt glacier**.

Follow the path on the north side of the Zmutt stream down to the small picturesque settlement of Zmutt and continue on this side of the valley down to **Zermatt**.

Comment: you can reach the Schönbiel hut (open in summer) in about 1¼ hrs over the lateral moraine of the Zmutt glacier amidst the most glorious landscape. Mountaineers use this hut as a base for high alpine walks to the Dent Blanche, the Tête de Valpelline, the Dent d'Hérens or for the Zmutt ridge on the Matterhorn.

36 Platthorn, 3345m and Mettelhorn, 3406m

Demanding summit walk with overwhelmingly beautiful views

Zermatt – Alterhaupt – Trift mountain hut – Platthorn/Mettelhorn – Zermatt

Location and starting point: Zermatt, 1616m. Your starting point is the Zermatt station of the BVZ. Big pay car park in Täsch. Frequent service of the BVZ Täsch-Zermatt between about 6.30 and 23.00, about 11 minute journey. Free parking for train passengers at Visp station (about an hourly service and a 1¼ hr journey).

Walking times: Zermatt – Trift mountain hut 2¼ hrs, Trift mountain hut – Platthorn about 3 hrs, descent to Zermatt 3 – 3½ hrs.

Ascent: 1730m to the Platthorn, 1790m to the Mettelhorn.

Grade: very long walk into high alpine country. You can shorten the long ascent by staying overnight in the Trift mountain hut. The path over the flat glacier to the Mettelhorn summit has become more difficult over the last years with an increasing number of crevisses opening up. The Mettelhorn should only be climbed in suitable conditions and with high alpine equipment (about another 30 minute climb).

Stops and accommodation: Alterhaupt (Hotel Edelweiss), 1961m. Trift mountain hut, 2337m (also overnight stops), tel: 079/4087020.

Worth seeing: picturesque ravine of the Trift stream, with beautiful flowers, as far as the Trift mountain hut. Popular viewing point at Alterhaupt. In good weather (and this walk should only be undertaken then) the view of the mountains of the Zermatt valley basin is truly spectacular, especially of the east face of the Zinalrothorn and the south side of the Weißhorn.

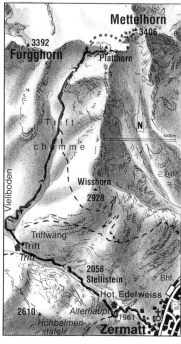

It is recommended that you make an overnight stop in the Trift mountain hut for this unusually long walk. Only undertake the walk in safe weather conditions.

Ascent to the Trift mountain hut: from **Zermatt station** follow the main road into the village centre. The path turns off right at a signpost and goes up

View from Gornergrat to the Weißhorn – the Mettelhorn is directly below, the Platt-horn is a little to the left below the Schalijoch.

westwards across the meadow slopes to the Trift gorge where the track has been blasted into the rocks for a short way. Then go over the bridge and wind your way up steeply to the **Alterhaupt** hotel. The path now crosses less steeply into the gorge where it changes over onto the other side at the narrowest point near the Stellistein and eventually leads across meadow slopes full of flowers to the **Trift mountain hut**.

Continuing to the Platthorn: from the mountain hut follow the path for about another 400m into the valley in the direction of the Rothorn hut and at Vieliboden turn off right (signpost) to climb over the grassy ridge into Triftchumme.

The vegetation gradually becomes more sparse and you reach, over scree slopes, the upper hollow west of the Platthorn. The track – sometimes over old snowfields – goes to the right across the col between the Platthorn and the Furgghorn (waymarkers). Continue eastwards on tracks through the scree to the **Platthorn**.

Return on the ascent path.

Six day walk around Zermatt

High above the Zermatt basin for a week

Täsch – Täschalp – Fluealp – Gornergrat – Riffelberg – Schwarzsee – Trift mountain hut – Zermatt

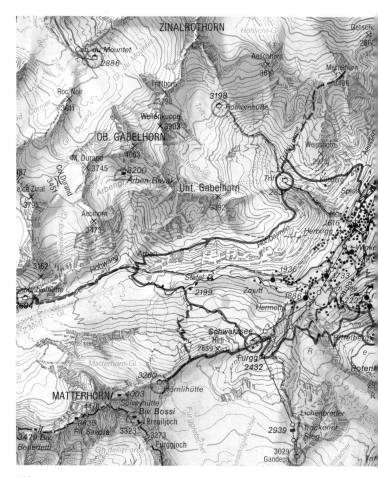

Zermatt offers a special treat for walkers. By putting together Walks 32 to 36 you can circumnavigate the whole of the Zermatt basin in a week and stop overnight in good accommodation (every establishment offers full-board) after a day of not too strenuous walking. A fast descent into the valley is possible at practically any point of the round walk.

Route:

Day 1: Täsch – Täschalp – Tifteren – Sunnegga – Fluealp hut (2618m, open almost all year round, rooms and bunks, tel: 027/9672597. 5 – 6 hrs, see Walk 32. **Day 2**: Fluealp – Grindjisee – Grünsee hut (accommodation, tel. 02/9672553 – Kulm hotel at Gornergrat mountain station (3131m, open almost all year round, rooms, tel: 027/9666400. 3 hrs. **Day 3**: Kulm hotel at Gornergrat – Gornergrat glacier – Rotenboden – Riffelberg (2566m, hotel, open summer and winter, rooms, tel: 027/9666500) or Riffelalp mountain hotel (2200m, renovation due to be completed in 2000, tel: 027/9664646). 2 – 3 hrs to the Riffelberg, ½ further to Riffelalp, see also Walk 34. **Day 4**: Riffelberg/Riffelalp – Gorner glacier tongue/glacier garden – Furgg – Hotel Schwarzsee (2584m, rooms, tel: 027/9672263). 3½ hrs. **Day 5**: Schwarzsee – Stafelalp – Arben – Höhbalmen – Trift mountain hut (2337m, open in summer, rooms and bunks, tel: 079/4087020). 4 hrs, see Walk 35. Detour from the Zmutt glacier to the Schoenbiel hut possible (ascent takes a good hour, return ¾ hr). **Day 6**: another detour to the Platthorn possible (ascent 3 hrs, descent 2 hrs, see Walk 35). Trift mountain hut – Flue – Chüeberg – Zermatt. 1½ – 2 hrs.

37 Schali (»Arigscheis«), 2243m

Little known and varied walk with exceptionally good views

Täsch – »Arigscheis« – Schalenäbi – Täsch

Location and starting point: Täsch, 1450m, BVZ stop, frequent service to Visp, and to Zermatt especially. Pay car park in Täsch, no parking in the village except for hotel guests. Your starting point is the station.

Walking times: Täsch – Arigscheis 2½ hrs, detour to the Schali glacier and back 1 hr, descent to Täsch 2 hrs.

Ascent: 800m, 900m on the detour to the glacier.

Highest point: Arigscheis, 2243m, but about 2350m on the glacier detour.

Grade: walk with a few short and somewhat exposed sections. Path marked throughout. No refreshments on the way. Restaurants in Täsch.

Worth seeing: interesting path over the very steep and at times rocky flank above Täsch with wonderful larch trees (particularly beau-

tiful in autumn). From below it seems impossible that there's a good path through here! Interesting views across the valley over to Täschalp and Alphubel, in the other direction to the Weisshorn and the chaotically broken Schali glacier.

Go over the bridge behind **Täsch station** and after a few metres out of the valley you reach the turn-off onto a path (signpost). The path zigzags up through the steep larch wood directly above Täsch, where it leads deftly between rocks and sometimes gets a little airy (at one point a ladder has been erected). The wood thins out further up and is interspersed with Swiss pines. With magnificent views just above the treeline, follow the path, almost on the level, to the **»Arigscheis«** viewing point (jokers have put a nameplate up just underneath!).

It's worth taking a detour along the path which leads at about the same height onto **the Schali glacier,** where the views of the surrounding mountains like the Zinalrothorn and Weißhorn are out of this world. However you should return as far as »Arigscheis« because rocks blocking the way make the direct descent to the Schalenäbi almost impossible.

Return to Täsch: from Arigscheis the good path goes down across the side of the valley south of the Schali stream to Schalenäbi, an area of alpine meadows with boulders and a few Swiss pines and larch trees. Shortly

From »Arigscheis« there's a fantastic view into the Schali glacier basin.

before you reach the gorge of the stream itself the path leaves the valley, eventually through dense forest again, and finally winds down to the Vispa valley bottom. Walk about 1.5km back to Täsch along a fairly level roadway parallel to the Vispa.

38 Weißhorn hut, 2932m

Long hut walk to the starting point for the normal ascent of one of the most beautiful mountains in the Alps

Randa – Rötiboden – Jatz – Weißhorn hut

Location and starting point: Randa, 1407m, stop for the BVZ railway, frequent service to Visp as well as Täsch/Zermatt.
Walking times: Randa – Rötiboden 1½ hrs, to Jatz 1 hr, rest of the ascent to the hut 2 hrs, total time about 4½ hrs.
Ascent: 1500m.
Grade: good and sufficiently marked mountain path.
Stops and accommodation: Weißhorn hut, open from the middle of July to the

beginning/middle of September (inquire in the tourist office or at the hut itself, tel: 027/9671262). If you should plan an overnight stop at the hut it is especially important to telephone the warden so that over-occupancy can be avoided if possible.
Worth seeing: idyllic views from the Dom and Täschhorn and into the Schali glacier basin. The ascent as far as Jatz goes across a steep flank with great views into the Matter valley.

From the hamlet of Täschberg you can see the whole of the hut path below the Weißhorn.

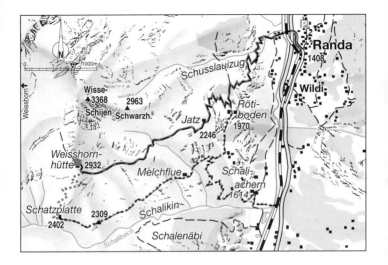

Go a few steps from **Randa** station to the north and over the Vispa bridge. You come past the Eien huts (on the right the mound of debris from the rock fall of 1991), then the steep mountain path begins. Go up round a few bends, then into a steep U-shaped valley and afterwards into the mountain forest.

After about 45 minutes, at the edge of a cliff, there's a great view into the valley and the path curves round to the ledge opposite, the Rötiboden, with good views too. The path continues up steeply to the Jatz alpine hut, where even the fittest hiker will eventually need to take a rest, before the path turns up onto the higher slopes of the Hohlicht.

Still ascending, you go diagonally across the steep grass slopes on a good path into a side valley, round a ledge, continue upwards near to some rocks until eventually you reach the last sweat-making final climb, zigzagging up to the visible **Weißhorn hut** above – as a hiker you can console yourself with the fact that »Weisshorn aspirants« here have to carry up quite different rucksacks.

The **return** generally follows the ascent path.

At the time of going to press there were the markings for work on an earlier path used by alpinists from the Weisshorn down to the Schatzplatte on the Höhlicht glacier. Work should be finished soon – the hut walk will then be extended into an interesting round walk (information from the hut warden and in the tourist office of Randa).

39 Moosalp- Jungen

Interesting ridge path in the Augstbord region

Moosalp – Augstbordstafel – Jungen – St. Niklaus

Location: Zeneggen, 1374m, Bürchen, 1200-1650m, post bus service from Visp (up to 12 buses a day). Törbel, 1497m, post bus service from Stalden (about 14 buses a day). St. Niklaus, 1116m, small cable-car to Jungen (Jungu).

Starting point: Moosalp, 2048m, broad alpine col on the high ridge between Zeneggen, Bürchen and Törbel. Road from these communities, post bus service (3 to 5 buses a day).

Walking times: Moosalp – Augstbordstafel 2 hrs, further on to Jungen 1½ hrs, descent to St. Niklaus 1½ hrs.

Ascent: 300m, descent 1100m.

Highest point: about 2200m on the section Augstbordstafel – Jungen.

Grade: good, broad path up to Läger, then at times exposed mountain path.

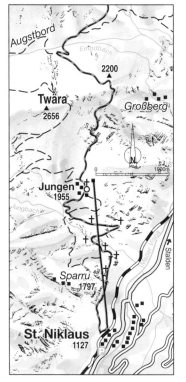

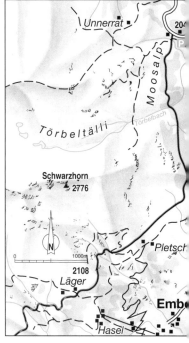

View from Jungen of the Balfrin and Nadelhorn mountains.

Kapellenweg from Jungen to St. Niklaus.
Stops and accommodation: Restaurants on the Moosalp and in Jungen.
Worth seeing: the wonderfully situated villages of Zeneggen, Törbel and Embd.

High ridge of the Moosalp, great views, especially from the Standbiel and Goldbiel. Jungen lies in a marvellous position – high above the Matter valley, opposite the Mischabelrange.

The Augstborderi is one of the historic aqueducts in the Valais. 18km long, it channels the water out of the Augstbord valley as far as Zeneggen. Over the centuries it has been rebuilt four times. Today's version dates from 1940.

Start at **Moosalp** car park and walk almost on the level into the larch wood. Later, as you reach open pasture land, continue a few metres uphill where the Mischabel range opposite comes well into view. The path first of all goes along meadow slopes amidst delightful scenery then through two short dark tunnels.

Passing above Läger of the Rieberg you have to descend 100m onto a path which crosses further below. Follow this through two gullies of broken rock on the very steep grassy slopes till you reach **Augstbordstafel**. After a bend on the opposite slope the ridge path to Jungen branches off left. Take this to cross the north slope below Twära until you come to a corner high above the Matter valley with beautiful views.

The following section of the walk has been built across an exciting steep slope which, from the distance, seems totally inaccessible. You soon reach the pretty settlement of Jungen. For those who would like to continue or are unsure about taking the tiny cable-car down into the valley, there's a well-laid path down through magnificent trees to St. Niklaus – this path has been constructed only recently as a chapel path (Kapellenweg).

40 Zeneggen vineyard

Descent into the vineyards

Zeneggen – Esch – Riedboden – Vispa – Neubrück/Stalden

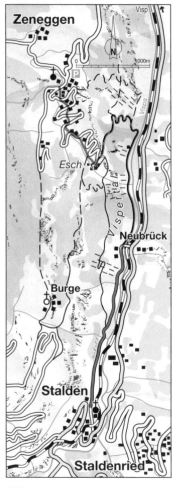

Location: Visp, 651m. Junction in the Rhone valley with very good train and bus connections. Parking in Visp and Zeneggen, then return by bus or Zermatt railway (BVZ).

Starting point: Zeneggen, 1374m. Small, pretty holiday resort in sunny position with fantastic views of the surrounding summits – Bietschhorn, Weißmies and Mischabel. Bus connection from Visp and across the Moosalp from Stalden/Törbel.

Walking times: Zeneggen – Esch ¾ hr, Esch – Riedboden ¾ hr, descent into the valley ¾ hr, return to Neubrück 30 minutes. Total time about 2½ hrs.

Descent: 700m.

Highest point: Zeneggen bus parking area, 1374m.

Stops and accommodation: restaurants in Zeneggen, Stalden and Visp.

Worth seeing: old Zeneggen, Biel chapel, restored mill at the Alpenblick hotel.

Well-cared for vineyards, but also many untended. Bouldering area below the village. Visp and Stalden with their old town centres.

A walk without any uphill climbing from the village down into the Vispa valley. Take the old, little-used path through various hamlets, some still inhabited, as far as Esch. After a few steps you come to a steep precipice which separates the village from the mountain vineyards (Driest). In an aesthetically pleasing way the path surmounts the horizontal steep terrace, leads into the forest and re-

The narrow Zeneggen mountain vineyard drops down steeply into the Vispa valley.

aches the Zenegger mountain vineyards facing southeast. Unfortunately many of them have been left untended. In those vineyards still in use, 8 different sorts of vine are cultivated, amongst them, the Heida, the oldest one in the Valais.

From the car park near the church in **Zeneggen** go along the tarmac road 150m south as far as the fork in the road. Continue down the lovely old path of paving stones between houses. The new tarmac road repeatedly crosses the areas of Egga, Widum, Sisetsch, Trolera, Rieder to **Esch**. Turn off here to the north and towards a steep cliff. Descend a skillfully laid path on horizontal rocks down into the forest and to the vineyards called **Riedboden**. Descend right (eastwards) along a small sandy road which eventually reaches the **Vispa**. Do not go over the bridge, instead go right and along the pathway by the river and to **Neubrück** (BVZ stop) or further on to **Stalden** along the old road.

Alternative: from Stalden to Visp on the newly constructed planetary path (length of the path:solar system 1:1 000 000 000, about 4.5km).

41 Augstbordhorn, 2973m

High above the Rhône and Vispa valleys

Moosalp – March – Augstbordhorn – Törbeltälli – Moosalp

Location: Törbel, 1497m, small village high above Stalden on the sunburned southern slope of the Moosalp. Bürchen, 1200 – 1650m, hamlet situated on the north side below the Moosalp.

Starting point: Moosalp, 2048m, broad ridge between Törbel and Bürchen with high moors and magnificent larch trees. Post bus connection with about 3 buses a day from Bürchen and 5 from Törbel.

Walking times: Moosalp – March 2¾ hrs, March – Augstbordhorn ¾ hrs, return (possibly through Törbeltälli) a good 2 hrs.

Ascent: 980m to the Augstbordhorn, 830m

onto the March.

Grade: easy mountain walk on marked paths which go almost up to 3000m, where there can still be snow, even in summer.

Stops and accommodation: restaurant on Moosalp (Chalte Brunne).

Worth seeing: the March range of mountains offers wonderful views deep into the Rhône valley and of the Bernese Alps opposite with the Bietschhorn towering above. From the Augstbordhorn you can also see the Weißhorn range and across the Vispa valleys there's a lovely view into the Mischabel mountains.

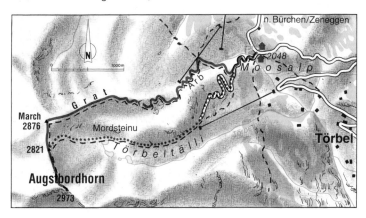

From the Chalte Brunne restaurant on **Moosalp** you walk along the roadway westwards at first through a light larch tree wood, then uphill across open alpine meadows. Leave the roadway running left into the Törbeltälli and climb up steeply close to the ski lifts (Arb) to the ridge and with a wonderful panorama, follow this as far as the **March**.

Autumn on Moosalp – knotty, weathered larch trees and interesting views.

The good path goes for a short way southwards into the cleft, 2821m, between the two summits and then through boulders over the north ridge onto the **Augstbordhorn**. The **descent** follows either the ascent path or goes directly into the **Törbeltälli** between March and Augstbordhorn.

Leave the connecting ridge to the March close to its deepest point and climb the first 100m over boulders and gravel, then partly along tracks to the Mordsteinu in the Törbeltälli with its small pretty lake. Near to the skilift station you come to the roadway which you take to return easily to **Moosalp**.

42 From Ergisch into the Turtmann valley

Quiet walk along an aqueduct - »path of the eagles«

Ergisch – Hübschweidi – Alpe Alpetjini – Obermatte – Ergisch

Location and starting point: Ergisch, 1086m, accessible along a narrow road from Turtmann, post bus connection (about 8 buses a day, 22 minute journey).

Walking times: Ergisch – Turtmann valley/Hübschweidi 1¾ hrs, ascent to Alpe Alpetjini 1¾ hrs, descent to Ergisch 1 hr.

Ascent: 700m.

Highest point: Alpe Alpetjini, 1770m.

Grade: mountain walk on good paths with some very exposed sections.

Stops and accommodation: Hübschweidi restaurant, situated a little way above the route of this walk on the Turtmann valley road (detour about 10 minutes).

Worth seeing: even the aqueduct from the Turtmann valley had to be cut into the rock faces in places or goes across steep forest slopes. It channels the water of the Turtmänna into the meadows and fields of Ergisch. Beautiful views from the Alpe Alpetjini into the Turtmann valley and onto the top of the glacier around the Weißhorn. In Ergisch you can find a lovely collection of old Valais houses. Along the path you will find information about the life of the eagles living here.

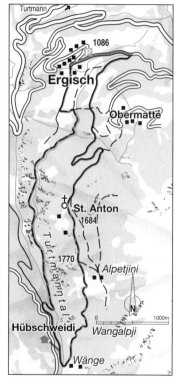

From the centre of **Ergisch** you go a short way to the upper roadway which crosses the meadow slopes as it goes into the valley. After about 600m a steep path branches off, surrounded by thick bushes, (signpost). For just under 100m you have a strenuous climb until you reach the aqueduct and the effortless part of the walk can begin. Always keeping alongside the water, you walk past steep rock faces, through thick mountain forests, then over steep dry slopes with little vegetation. Gradually as you approach the valley bottom the sound of the Turtmänna gets louder and louder and it is channelled across a bridge at the small reservoir. After a while the path goes up to the old Turtmann valley forest track which you now continue to follow into the valley, always just below the road and at the same time below the **Hübschweidi** restaurant. After one kilometre the path turns off left and crosses the stream again – just before this you can turn off right and reach the restaurant in 10 minutes.

After the bridge the path climbs gradually through the forest at first then after a small clearing winds very steeply upwards and crosses the flank to the open alpine meadow slopes of **Alpetjini**. Here you come to a rough forest track which soon brings you past St. Anton chapel and round wide bends through the forest to **Obermatte** and eventually back to **Ergisch**.

In some places the water channel is cut into the rock face.

43 Meid pass, 2790m

From the Turtmann valley into the wildly romantic Meidtälli with its eight lakes

Gruben-Meiden – Meidealp – Meid pass

Location and starting point: Gruben-Meiden, 1822m, in the upper Turtmann valley.
Walking times: Gruben – Meidealp 1½ hrs, to the Meid pass 1½ hrs, return into the valley 2 hrs.
Ascent: 970m.
Grade: easy mountain walk on good path, sufficiently marked.
Stops and accommodation: restaurant in Gruben-Meiden. No facilities en route.
Worth seeing: the Turtmann valley is the only largish side valley of the Rhône in the

Valais which has remained practically undeveloped for tourists. Apart from alpine farming and a small water works there is no significant human intrusion into nature. Previously, quite small ore mines were worked. The walk in this quiet valley is in complete contrast to other objectives. However, it is full of interest here. There are small lakes with their varied colour tones complimented by the splendid view of the Weißhorn, all providing an optimum alpine enjoyment.

The path begins at the hamlet of **Gruben-Meiden** and straight away goes over the stream, the Turtmänna, and then shortly afterwards turns off right before the next houses. Going pleasantly uphill, alternately through mountain forest and over open ground, the path goes up across the steep terrace,

Rock needle on the Meidspitz above the Meidtälli and the lake of the same name.

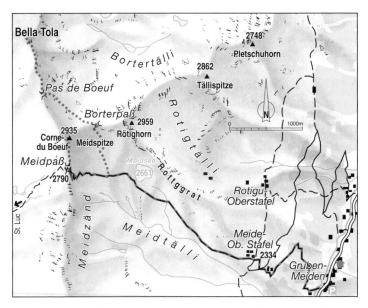

then, above a small rocky area, crosses over the forest boundary to the nice **alpine settlement of Meide** Mittel Stafel and after crossing the roadway, to Ober Stafel, where it's worth taking a good rest. The Weißhorn looks like a sharp needle from here. The path now goes easily uphill far into the Meidtälli – the weathered rock towers of Meidzänd stand impressively at the far end above multi-coloured fields of rubble. After a short terrace you come past the Meid lake then make your last traverse over scree, here too in beautiful colour tones, and you reach the **Meid pass** round a few bends. Together with the view of the whole of the Turtmann valley you can see across the wide expanses of meadows and debris in the direction of St. Luc in the Val d'Anniviers.

For climbers there are routes on the Meidspitz southern summit (grade II). Those who feel totally unstretched should turn off the ascent to the top of the pass along an unclear path just before the uppermost scree slopes going upwards to the right (cairn) to the nearby Borter pass and climb further on up to the Pas de Boeuf and the famous Bella Tola (1½ hrs) – certainly the most beautiful approach to this panoramic mountain since a skiing area has considerably spoilt the other side.

Return down the ascent path.

44 Blüomatt – Turtmann valley

Peaceful walk with good views of the Weißhorn

Blüomatt (Turtmann valley) – Chalte Berg (Blüomatt-Tälli) – Turtmann reservoir – Vorderer Sänntum – Blüomatt

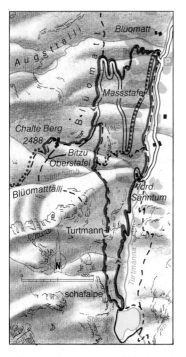

Location: Gruben-Meiden, 1822m, uppermost village, in the Turtmann valley only inhabited in summer. Cable-car from Turtmann to Oberems at the end of the valley. Bus.

Starting point: Blüomatt, 1863m, alpine meadow settlement about 1km south from Gruben-Meiden. Parking at the bridge over the Turtmänna near Blüomatt.

Walking times: Blüomatt – Chalte Berg 2 hrs, Chalte Berg ridge path – Turtmann reservoir 1 hr, valley descent to Blüomatt 2¼ hrs.

Ascent: 670m.

Highest point: Chalte Berg, 2488m.

Grade: easy walk on well marked paths. No facilities en route.

Worth seeing: there are beautiful views on this walk of the Weißhorn mountains and the area of the Turtmann hut around the Brunegg and Turtmann glaciers.

In earlier times there has been mining in this valley and you can still see traces of this in some places. Up to now the Turtmann valley has been little known and offers really solitary walks away from the hubbub of tourists in the neighbouring valleys and on top you will find particularly interesting flora.

There's a track going up to the Chalte Berg mountain pasture, but you turn off right just behind the bridge towards a group of houses (signpost, the actual settlement of **Blüomatt** lies another good 300m further north). Zigzag up through the beautiful mountain forest to the Mass Stafel alpine meadow where you meet the track again. You can take a shortcut from one of the bends on a path across the meadows full of flowers, then you follow the narrow road, as if on a viewing terrace, southwards as it gently ascends into the Blüomatt-Tälli. On the last few metres you take the footpath again

Bishorn and Weißhorn from the Blüomatt alpine meadows.

straight up to the huts of **Chalte Berg**.

Descent: the easiest way is to go back down along the ascent path or the track (1 to 1¼ hrs). But it's more interesting to take the gently descending ridge path above the Turtmann valley along to the reservoir of the same name below the Turtmann glacier.

For this you turn off about half way between Chalte Berg and Mass-Stafel. After a few bends the path leads past Bitzu-Oberstafel (steep descent) over the Sänntum stream and then almost on the level southwards as far as the small Turtmann reservoir. It's a nice easy walk along the track through the valley to the Vorderen Sänntum, the end of the used road. On the west side of the Turtmänna the track goes back to Blüomatt and the road runs to the east of it.

45 Lötschen valley ridge path

Marvellous high altitude walk with grand views of the Bietschhorn

Fafleralp – Tellistafel – Lauchernalp – Wiler

Location: Kippel, 1376m, main village of the Lötschen valley. Good post bus connections with Gampel/Steg (Rhône valley) via Goppenstein (station of the Lötschberg line).
Starting point: Fafleralp, 1787m, small settlement at he furthermost point of the Lötschen valley, end station of the post bus in the summer, large car park.
Walking times: Fafleralp – Tellistafel 1 hr, Tellistafel – Lauchernalp 1½ hrs.
Ascent: 320m, or 460m respectively.
Highest point: about 2100m, before the Lauchernalp, or 2239m (Arbächnubel).

Grade: easy mountain walk on good, marked paths.
Stops and accommodation: several restaurants on Lauchernalp.
Worth seeing: the Lötschen valley is still one of the quiet side valleys of the Rhône that has remained in its truly original state, with beautiful villages.
Alpine meadows covered in flowers, views from the area of the forest boundary of the high ice summits, especially the Bietschhorn. Lötschen valley museum in Kippel.

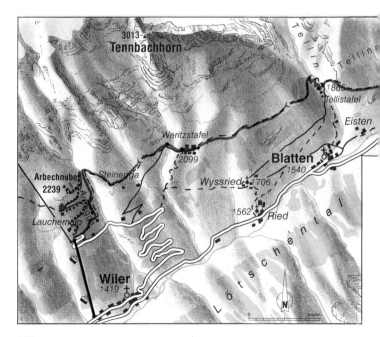

Autumn colours on the Lötschen valley ridge path.

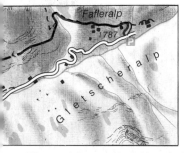

This justiiably famous ridge walk can be extended (45 minutes, see Walk 47) as far as Kummenalp (restaurant).

From the bus stop at the Gletscherstafel car park go a few metres northwards in the direction of Inners valley and then along the track to reach the houses of **Fafleralp**. Continue below the edge of the wood on the level into the Uisters (outer) valley, out on the other side again and uphill round the wooded ridge to the Schwarz lake, a popular and very photogenic resting place. The good path continues, still hardly uphill, into the valley »Im Tellin«. At the huts of **Tellistafel**, 1865m, the ridge now branches off right from the track which leads to Wyssried, through the forest to the alpine meadows above. Go gradually uphill across this viewing terrace to the Weritzstafel huts, 2099m. Follow the track only as far as across the Tänn stream, then shortly after the ridge branches off again right, past Steinegga into the cleft of the Mili stream. The direct path leads down to Arbegga and only on the last few metres along the narrow road to the mountain station of **Lauchernalp** cable-car.

However it's worth climbing to the viewing point Arbächnubel, 2239m, a short way up from the Mili stream! Take the cable-car to **Wiler** or descend on foot in 1¼ hrs.

46 Bietschhorn hut, 2565m

A walk amidst natural landscape to an isolated hut

Ried near Blatten – Nestalp – Howitzen – Bietschhorn hut

Location and starting point: Ried in the Lötschen valley, 1486m, small village near Blatten with several old houses.

Bus stop of the Goppenstein – Fafleralp route (almost hourly buses, 20 minute journey).

Walking times: Ried – Nestalp 2 hrs, ascent via Howitzen to the hut 2 hrs, return 2½ hrs.

Ascent: 1080m.

Grade: easy mountain walk on good paths, the crossing of the Nest stream over large boulders can require at most something of a balancing act (if you want to bypass this you can climb directly up from Wiler through

the mountain forest to above the stream crossing).

Stops and accommodation: Bietschhorn hut of the Bernese Academic Alpine Club. From time to time in the season there's a warden there who provides drinks and simple meals. Inquire in the valley.

Worth seeing: the walk goes out of the Löschen valley through the high wooded area over the steep mountain slope into the barren, but geologically very interesting region at the northern end of the Bietschhorn mountains – the area below the Nesthorn glacier is especially impressive.

From **Ried** you go a few metres into the valley along the road and then right, across the stream and over the meadows of Birchmatte to the mountain

The Bietschhorn rises up into the storm clouds above the Bietschhorn hut.

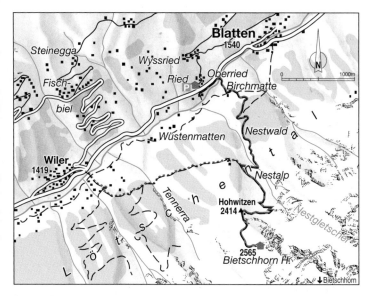

forest. The small path goes steeply up through this beautiful high forest and just above the gorge of the Nest stream reaches open terrain. In this **Nestalp** area the path continues steeply up through fields of bilberries and low bushes as it approaches the sound of rushing water.

At a suitable place you can usually cross the stream easily with the help of large stones – it can only become difficult shortly after rainfall and when the snow is melting. A few metres further up you meet the ascent path from Wiler – a possible alternative if you would prefer to avoid the stream crossing. Bleak moraine country typifies the surroundings of the next section as it becomes more »alpine« and you can hardly imagine how a normal path could continue up out of this basin.

A strip along a geological stratification suddenly makes it possible and with fantastic views, you reach the **Howitzen** ledge where there's a view into the next cirque and of the hut, now not far away. Continue a while along the »Howitz ridge« then over debris and finally along a grassy spur you climb up to the **Bietschhorn** hut – the Bietschhorn again towers up above the rocky landscape on this last section.

The **return** is back down the ascent route.

47 Jeizinen – Kummenalp

Ridge path above the outer Lötschen valley

Jeizinen – Fäsilalp – Faldumalp – Kummenalp – Ferden

Location: Gampel, 635m, village in the Rhône valley at the end of the Lötschen valley. Station of the SBB line in the Rhône valley (just to the south of the village), bus connection into the Lötschen valley.

Starting point: Jeizinen, 1526m, settlement high above the confluence of the Lötschen and Rhône valleys. Cable-car connection from Gampel-Steg. Service all year round, about every hour between 7.00 and 21.00.

Destination: Ferden, 1375m, in the Lötschen valley, regular post bus connection with Gampel via Goppenstein in the Rhône valley.

Walking times: Jeizinen – Fäsilalp 1½ hrs, ridge path to Faldumalp 2 hrs, continuing to Kummenalp 1 hr, descent to Ferden 1 hr.

Ascent: 800m.

Highest point: Heruhubel, 2308m.

Grade: easy and unproblematic, but a long walk on good paths.

Stops and accommodation: restaurants on Fäsilalp and Kummenalp, as well as in Jeizinen and Ferden.

Worth seeing: interesting journey up with small cable-car over the dry slopes of the Rhône valley. Idyllic views of the Valais Alps, especially of the Weißhorn mountains. As the walk progresses the views improve of the Lötschen valley and the Bietschhorn which towers up above.

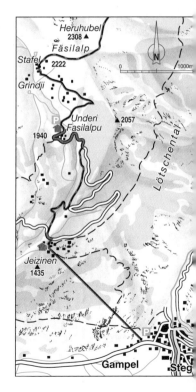

Up till now this ridge path above the Lötschen valley has been much less known than the ridge path described in Walk 45, so it's quite nice to do the walk on your own. It would be ideal to combine these two walks into a two day walk (see illustration on page 16).

From the mountain station of the Jeizinen cable-car you go for a short way through the village to the road, turn left and then immediately onto the path in the forest up the trench

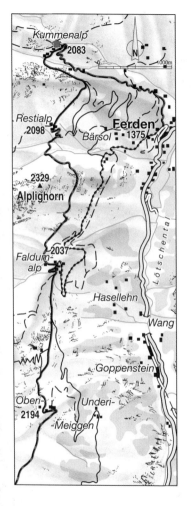

to the lower Fäsilalp, 1940m, a small settlement of alpine and holiday houses with a restaurant in the certainly unnecessary lift area – you can also get here by car along the tarmac road.

The continuing alpine track now leads round a big bend to the upper **Fäsilalp**, also called Stafel, 2222m. Here, above the forest boundary, you have an open view of the western Valais Alps. After the short climb to the Heruhubel the view opens out to the east and down into the Lötschen valley.

The path now goes into the valley with marvellous views, eventually past Alpe Oberi Meiggu – there's a particularly beautiful resting place here – and then crosses the steep slope with its avalanche barriers to **Faldumalp**, 2037m.

Only if you are in a hurry should you descend directly to Ferden on the track, otherwise it's definitely worth a short detour past Resigalp to **Kummenalp**, 2083m, with restaurant.

You can see the whole length of the Lötschen valley from here and the enormous triangular Bietschhorn. which towers above, dominating everything.

The **descent** is either along the track or a more interesting and beautiful alternative is to take the footpath, at times steep, directly down to **Ferden**.

Return to Gampel in the Rhône valley by post bus via Goppenstein.

48 Rhône valley – Erschmatt

Dry biotope and bold bridge construction over the gorge

Getwing – Hohe Brücke (»devil's bridge«) – Erschmatt – Getwing

Location and starting point: Getwing, 626m, several small sections of village in the Rhône valley, at the foot of the dry slopes of the Bernese Alps between Leuk and the Lötschen valley opposite Turtmann.

Walking times: Getwing – Hohe Brücke ¾ hr, Hohe Brücke – Erschmatt 1 hr, descent to Getwing 1¼ hrs.

Ascent: 600m.

Highest point: Erschmatt hamlet, 1228m. Beautiful village centre.

Grade: easy walk on marked paths.

Stops and accommodation: in Erschmatt.

Worth seeing: interesting dry slope vegetation with the Perücken bush which turns fire-red in autumn. Hohe Brücke (Teufelsbrücke) over the very narrow, but deep gorge of the Feschel stream. The new bridge is just below the old one, breathtakingly daring in its construction, about which there are similar legends to those of the Schöllenen gorge on the Gotthard route.

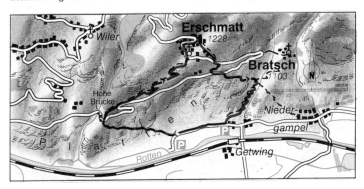

This walk is especially worthwhile in early summer and into late autumn when the first snow is already on the mountain tops. On the other hand, because of its southerly location, it can turn out to be unbelievably thirst-making.

From Unter-**Getwing** go along the narrow road through some areas of vine and fruit cultivation a good 600m down the Rhône. Your path turns off right where the road bends left towards the river, crosses a bridge over a water ditch and then climbs up right across the valley slope (»Platten«). The vegetation is here well suited to the extreme aridity and direct sunlight, the colours of the Perücken bush in autumn almost seem unreal – whole areas of the slope turn fire-red.

When you reach the mountain road you must be sure to go the few metres left to the **Hohe Brücke**. Here you can marvel at the old art of bridge building

Fire-red autumn colours of the Perückenstrauch (wig bush) on the ascent to Hohe Brücke.

– especially in this boldly exposed place. The path from here cuts off two bends of the road and then follows the old cart track as far as **Erschmatt**. On the way you cross an area of recent forest fire where plants, quite different to the ones that appear on the dry slopes immediately next to them, have started to grow.

Descent: the path leaves Erschmatt down to the south east, crosses the road again and descends, in places quite steeply, but easily, to a small trench which comes down from the neighbouring village of Bratsch. Continue winding down the valley and you soon reach the first vineyards and eventually arrive back at **Getwing**.

49 Torrenthorn, 2998m

Outstanding vantage point on an »almost 3-thousander«

Rinder hut – Torrenthorn

Location and starting point: Leukerbad, 1402m, well-known sports' resort and spa in the upper valley of the Dala.

Bus connection almost every hour with Leuk (SBB railway station, a good 30 minute journey, 17km). Take a cable-car up to the Rinder hut, 2310m (on foot 2½ hrs), or alternatively go by bus from Leukerbad to Albinen and then by chairlift from Flaschen/Albinenleitern (on foot 1¼ hrs) up to the hut.

Walking times: Rinder hut – Torrenthorn 2¼ hrs, return 1¼ hrs.

Ascent: 690m.

Grade: easy mountain path at high altitude.

Stops and accommodation: in the Rinder hut (mountain station of the cable-car) and in the Torrenthorn hotel, situated about 30 minutes above the station on the path.

Worth seeing: the height and geographical location of this mountain certainly speak volumes – practically all of the Valais Alps stand opposite in a row. The north is dominated by the rock face of the Gemmi pass continuing on both sides to the Daubenhorn (left) and the Rinderhorn and Balmhorn (right). The peaks of the Blümlisalp and Jungfrau mountains rise up in the background.

The region is ideal for walkers and is famous for its particularly rich diversity of plants – hopefully the »ski developers« will remember this fact before the realisation of their plans for a ski association Leukerbad – Albinen!

From the **Rinder hut** cable-car station climb the good path to the Torrenthorn hotel close by – unfortunately, like the Rinder hut, not an architecturally

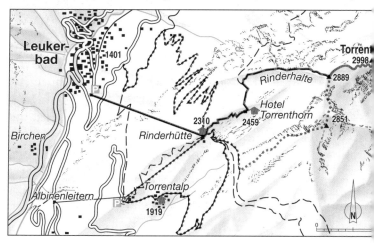

View down from the Torrenthorn to Leukerbad with the Gemmi pass above.

glittering performance. Here the path crosses the bare meadows of the Rinderhalte to the north onto the panoramic west ridge of the Torrenthorn along which it now continues. Even before the climb could become really strenuous you reach the broad first summit where the view now opens up of the middle section of the Valais Alps. Without great effort across the wide field of debris, you soon come to the **Torrenthorn** itself which quite unexpectedly drops away to the south and north with sheer broken rock faces and contrary to the scary last section, gives you a true summit feeling.

The **return** keeps to the ascent path. If you are confident about climbing on broken rocks and very sure-footed then you could also descend via the Schafberg on the other side of the first summit (some short scrambling sections on debris covered rock slabs), and then continue down westwards with no paths – on the right hand side the rock face falls away into the Torrent basin – until you meet the last section of the path from Bachalp.

50 Varneralp, 2200m

High above the Rhône and Dala valleys

Varen – Alpe Pfarschong – Varneralp

Location: Varen, 760m, wine growing village situated above the Rhône valley with beautiful views at the crossing point of the eastern into the western Valais. Bus connection with Sierre and Leuk.

Starting point: barrier sign on the alpine road above the campfire of the »Schweizer Familie« in the Varner forest, about 1530m, on foot about 2 hrs, but then the whole walk would be really long and exhausting! Drive from Varen by car towards Leukerbad-Rumeling. Directly behind the upper bend by the last houses a road branches off to the left (in the direction of Taschuniere). It's an asphalt road at first and then has a natural surface and winds round several bends to the barrier sign above the campfire.

Walking times: camp fire – Pfarschong mountain pasture 1¼ hrs, climb up to Varneralp about 1 hr.

Ascent: 670m.

Grade: easy mountain walk on good paths.

Stops and accommodation: restaurants in Varen, otherwise no facilities.

Worth seeing: beautiful views into the Rhône valley and the valley basin of Leukerbad with the surrounding peaks. What is more, you come into the areas on this walk where, at the end of the Ice Age, a large mass of rock slid down onto the retreating glacier and is preserved characteristically in the form of the hill of the Pfyn forest and also near to Sierre.

At the bend in the road from **Varen** above the campfire you have your first beautiful view into the Dala valley and down to Leukerbad. This is also where

Leuk, surrounded by vineyards, and behind it, the hillside up to Varneralp.

138

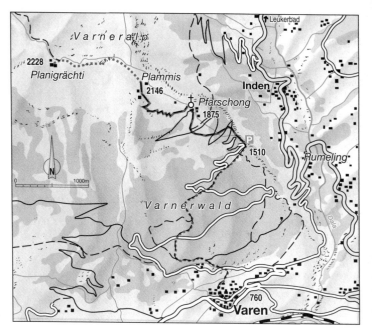

you have to leave your car. You can of course follow the track, but the narrow path is more varied and goes straight up across open terrain, passes another bend in the track which it then crosses several times before reaching the **Pfarschong** alpine meadow with its small chapel and some huts. A beautiful ridge path branches off here high above the Dala valley. At the top hut the path continues across barren meadows interspersed with broken rocky areas, now with open views of the Valais Alps and down into the Rhône valley.

The path goes diagonally up the flank and along an edge of the rock fall reaches the upper alpine meadows, the large terrace of **Varneralp**. Here too you will find an aqueduct which crosses the meadows and channels the water in this area. You should definitely walk another 15 minutes to the alpine buildings of Planigrächti, an especially beautiful vantage point high above the Rhône valley.

The **return** is back down the ascent route, but first, perhaps, you should make another detour with no paths to the eastern edge of the Varneralp, where a breathtaking view down to Leukerbad awaits.

Index

The numbers behind the headwords relate to the walk numbers or notes in the chapter »Locations« (L).